Dee

Nancy & I are
So Thankful That you
are a Sister in the Lord.

Steve

ONE CHRISTIAN'S PERSPECTIVE

OF

MAN'S DILEMMA

GOD'S SOLUTION

A work offered by
Steve Lampman
Email: Stevelampman@comcast.net
Website www.stevelampman.com

One Christian's Perspective Of Man's Dilemma
God's Solution
by Steve Lampman

Printed in the United States of America

ISBN 978-1-60647-282-8

About the Author

It was by the grace of God that Steve was brought to a saving faith in the Lord Jesus Christ. It was by God's longsuffering that he has been sustained in that faith. Steve became a Christian on November 17, 1961 when as a young marine on liberty he came upon a street meeting held by Open Air Campaigners for Christ in the city of Los Angeles, California. For the remaining three years of his enlistment after coming to faith, Steve immersed himself in various books and studies concerning his relationship with Christ.

During those three years he worshipped at Granada Heights Friends Church in La Mirada, CA. Sunday mornings and the Church of the Open Door in Los Angeles, CA. Sunday evenings. Steve was discipled by three families who were members of Granada Heights Friends Church and nurtured his faith. To these three families he will forever be grateful.

Those three years were a tremendous blessing to Steve, and it was the foundation gained in those three years that sustained him through several tumultuous years during which he walked away from a faithful walk with the Lord and lived as a prodigal son. But thanks to God, Steve was still a son, and as the prodigal of Luke 15:8-22 was never disowned by the Father. In 1985, after living a life of riotousness that almost destroyed him, Steve surrendered to the authority of God and has since been in service of his Lord and Savior, Jesus, the Christ. Steve readily acknowledges that it was and is only the grace of God that allowed him to remain alive during those years and by His love that Steve was brought back to fellowship with Him. This grace and love, Steve believes, is best spoken of in Romans 8:28-29:

"And we know that all things work together for the good of those who love him, who have been called according to his purpose. For those God foreknew he also predestined to be conformed to the likeness of his Son, that he might be the firstborn among many brothers. And those he predestined, he also called: those he called, he also justified: those he justified, he also glorified." (KJV)

It is confirmed in this passage that each child of God is being conformed (being changed) to the image of Jesus Christ. First, however, God calls that person out of the world into a loving relationship with Himself, making him a son. He justifies that person so that they may have fellowship one with the other and also that justification makes it possible for him to eventually be in the very presence of God.

TABLE OF CONTENTS

Chapter 1

Spiritual Darkness

A short time ago I overheard a conversation in which one of the conversationalists spoke several words of profanity. In the next breath, he talked about the men's group of the church of which he belonged. Granted, I don't know the man's heart, but something didn't seem to match up. I wondered how a man could take the Lord's name in vain and yet be a true Christian. Now, I am not suggesting that any of us is without sin. Each one of us sins every day by commission or omission. But it seemed by this man's language that this was his normal way of expression, and at best, was not respectful of the Lord, the One who suffered so greatly for the sake of mankind.

I wondered, "Is this man so blind that he doesn't realize that it is an affront to the Lord whenever His name is abused in this way? Is his heart so calloused that it doesn't bother him?" A calloused heart is for another consideration, but in this work we shall look at spiritual blindness, also known as spiritual darkness. Spiritual darkness in Scripture is used symbolically of ignorance and/or spiritual blindness. Certainly, man was not created this way; God Himself was satisfied with His creation. Man represented by Adam was created with a complete (mature) awareness of God. He was spiritually alive. In fact, in the creation account, we read that God endowed him with the ability to have dominion over the earth and all its inhabitants in accordance with God's will. This dominion was so complete that it reflected God's dominion over all creation. Consider Genesis 1:26-28: *"26Then God said, 'Let us make man in our image, in our likeness, and let them rule over the fish of the sea and the birds of the air, over the livestock, over all the earth, and over all the creatures that move along the ground.' 27 So God created man in his own image, in the image of God he created him; male and female he created them. 28God blessed them and said to them, 'Be fruitful and increase in number; fill the earth and subdue it. Rule over the fish of the sea and the birds of the air and over every living creature that moves on the ground.'"*

In addition, there was communication between Adam and God as seen in Genesis 2:8-17 and 3:8-13:

2:8-17 *"8Now the LORD God had planted a garden in the east, in Eden; and there he put the man he had formed. 9And the LORD God made all kinds of trees grow out of the ground—trees that were pleasing to the eye and good for food. In the middle of the garden were the tree of life and the tree of the knowledge of good* *and evil. ^{10} A river watering the garden flowed from Eden; from there it was separated into four headwaters. ^{11}The name of the first is the Pishon; it winds through the entire land of Havilah, where there is gold. ^{12}(The gold of that land is good; aromatic resin and onyx are also there.) ^{13}The name of the second river is the Gihon; it winds through the entire land of Cush. ^{14}The name of the third river is the Tigris; it runs along the east side of Asshur. And the fourth river is the Euphrates. ^{15}The LORD God took the man and put him in the Garden of Eden to work it and take care of it. ^{16}And the LORD God commanded the man, "You are free to eat from any tree in the garden; ^{17}but you must not eat from the tree of the knowledge of good and evil, for when you eat of it you will surely die."*

3:8-13 "^{8}Then the man and his wife heard the sound of the LORD God as he was walking in the garden in the cool of the day, and they hid from the LORD God among the trees of the garden. ^{9}But the LORD God called to the man, 'Where are you?' ^{10}He answered, 'I heard you in the garden, and I was afraid because I was naked; so I hid.' ^{11}And he said, 'Who told you that you were naked? Have you eaten from the tree that I commanded you not to eat from?' ^{12}The man said, 'The woman you put here with me—she gave me some fruit from the tree, and I ate it.' ^{13}Then the LORD God said to the woman, 'What is this you have done?' The *woman said, 'The serpent deceived me, and I ate.'"*

There are many points of theology contained in these two passages, but our consideration at this time is that of the fellowship and communication that existed between Lord God and Adam and Eve. Certainly, in the Garden before Adam's disobedience, spiritual darkness (blindness) did not exist. Adam was one with God in thought and deed. God's will was Adam's will. Adam's desire was to worship and please God. How, then, did it become a way of life to profane God in language and lifestyle? How did man become blind to God's holiness? How did he become delusional in thinking he could say or do as he pleased without consequence?

From Genesis, we learn that Adam disobeyed God and suffered immediate spiritual death (figurative for spiritual separation). Adam became so spiritually separated from holy God that God likened it to death. Just as physical death separates one from all that is living, so spiritual death separates one from God. This is why Jesus, in His dialogue with Nicodemus, said:

John 3:3 *" I tell you the truth, no one can see the kingdom of God unless he is born again."*

10

John 3:5-6 *"⁵I tell you the truth, no one can enter the kingdom of God unless he is born of water and the Spirit. ⁶Flesh gives birth to flesh, but the Spirit gives birth to spirit."*

Because of sin, man is not only dead toward and separated from God (bringing spiritual darkness), but is also alienated from Him. The progression of sin, commenced in Adam, was so drastic and rapid, that Adam and Eve's first offspring, Cain, because of jealousy and anger killed his brother Abel (Genesis 4:1-8). Spiritual darkness rapidly gripped the heart of Cain. He then rejected God's provision for the covering of sin, a sin offering that required shedding of blood. In spiritual darkness he thought to satisfy God's righteousness by instituting a sacrifice that was bloodless.

Even though there was a godly line of people who attempted to follow God through Seth, they were still willing to give their daughters to men who were not of the godly line, men possessed by fallen spirit beings. These unions produced offspring that became so wicked that God wiped all humanity off the face of the earth except the family of Noah.

Genesis 6:1-5 *"¹When men began to increase in number on the earth and daughters were born to them, [2]the sons of God saw that the daughters of men were beautiful, and they married any of them they chose. 3Then the LORD said, 'My Spirit will not contend with man forever, for he is mortal; his days will be a hundred and twenty years.' [4]The Nephilim (giants) were on the earth in those days—and also afterward—when the sons of God went to the daughters of men and had children by them. They were the heroes of old, men of renown. [5]The LORD saw how great man's wickedness on the earth had become, and that every inclination of the thoughts of his heart was only evil all the time."*

Oh, the depth of spiritual darkness! It resulted in spiritual death and separation. Without this spiritual death, Adam and Eve would not have lost the close relationship and fellowship they enjoyed with the Lord God in the Garden, Cain would not have killed his brother and unholy marriages would not have occurred. Spiritual death brought about wickedness so great that God destroyed all mankind except Noah and his family.

From Romans 1:18-23, we read of the conse-quence of spiritual death: *"[18]The wrath of God is being revealed from heaven against all the godlessness and wickedness of men who suppress the truth by their wickedness, [19]since what may be known about God is plain to them, because God has made it plain to them. [20]For since the creation of the world God's invisible qualities—his eternal power and divine nature—have been clearly seen, being understood from what has been made, so that men are without excuse. [21]For although they knew God, they neither glorified him as God nor gave thanks to him, but their thinking became futile and their foolish hearts were darkened. [22]Although they claimed to be wise, they became fools [23]and exchanged the glory of the immortal God for images made to look like mortal man and birds and animals and reptiles."* In this passage, Paul is referring to the unregenerate Gentile.

In his letter to the Ephesians Paul wrote that the wrath of God is toward all mankind. That all are guilty, Jew and Gentile, before God regenerates those He has chosen to new spiritual life. *"[1]As for you, you were dead in your transgressions and sins, [2]in which you used to live when you followed the ways of this world and of the ruler of the kingdom of the air, the spirit who is now at work in those who are disobedient. [3]All of us also lived among them at one time, gratifying the cravings of our sinful nature and following its desires and thoughts. Like the rest, we were by nature objects of wrath. [4]But because of his great love for us, God, who is rich in mercy, [5]made us alive with Christ even when we were dead in transgressions—it is by grace you have been saved" Ephesians 2:1-5.*

The natural propensity of man is to deny the very God they know exists and worship the creature. First Corinthians 2:14 explains: *"The man without the Spirit does not accept the things that come from the Spirit of God, for they are foolishness to him, and he cannot understand them, because they are spiritually discerned."* Spiritual darkness is the inability of the natural man to understand spiritual things, including but not limited to the truth that Jesus of Nazareth was the anointed of God.

Natural man cannot look at himself, his language, or his lifestyle with the eyes of God. Consider Jesus' dialogue in Matthew 15:1-20.

"¹Then some Pharisees and teachers of the law came to Jesus from Jerusalem and asked, ²Why do your disciples break the tradition of the elders? They don't wash their hands before they eat!' ³Jesus replied, 'And why do you break the command of God for the sake of your tradition?' ⁴For God said, 'Honor your father and mother' and 'Anyone who curses his father or mother must be put to death.' ⁵But you say that if a man says to his father or mother, 'Whatever help you might otherwise have received from me is a gift devoted to God,' ⁶he is not to 'honor his father' with it. Thus you nullify the word of God for the sake of your tradition. ⁷You hypocrites! Isaiah was right when he

prophesied about you: [8]'These people honor me with their lips, but their hearts are far from me. [9]They worship me in vain; their teachings are but rules taught by men.' [10]Jesus called the crowd to him and said, 'Listen and understand. [11]What goes into a man's mouth does not make him 'unclean,' but what comes out of his mouth, that is what makes him 'unclean.'' [12]Then the disciples came to him and asked, 'Do you know that the Pharisees were offended when they heard this?' [13]He replied, 'Every plant that my heavenly Father has not planted will be pulled up by the roots. [14]Leave them; they are blind guides. If a blind man leads a blind man, both will fall into a pit.' [15]Peter said, 'Explain the parable to us.' [16]'Are you still so dull?' Jesus asked them. [17]'Don't you see that whatever enters the mouth goes into the stomach and then out of the body? [18]But the things that come out of the mouth come from the heart, and these make a man 'unclean.'[19]For out of the heart come evil thoughts, murder, adultery, sexual immorality, theft, false testimony, slander. [20]These are what make a man 'unclean'; but eating with unwashed hands does not make him 'unclean.'''

Perhaps this explains why a person might have a religion, but not have a heart that is inclined to worship God or does not see anything wrong with slandering His holy name. Perhaps some believe this is just a way of expression and not really an act against

God, but isn't this line of thinking in contrast to what Jesus said in the above passage or what Paul was inspired to write in his letter to the Colossians? (Col. 3:5-10):

"5Put to death, therefore, whatever belongs to your earthly nature: sexual immorality, impurity, lust, evil desires and greed, which is idolatry. 6Because of these, the wrath of God is coming. 7You used to walk in these ways, in the life you once lived. 8But now you must rid yourselves of all such things as these: anger, rage, malice, slander, and filthy language from your lips. 9Do not lie to each other, since you have taken off your old self with its practices 10and have put on the new self, which is being renewed in knowledge in the image of its Creator."

The wrath of God will eventually be exacted against the unredeemed. All acts of sinful flesh, including filthy language, will be judged, and punishment will be exacted according to God's standards. Paul admonished the Ephesian believers (and us) to: *"1Be imitators of God, therefore, as dearly loved children 2and live a life of love, just as Christ loved us and gave himself up for us as a fragrant offering and sacrifice to God. 3But among you there must not be even a hint of sexual immorality, or of any kind of impurity, or of greed, because these are improper for God's holy people. 4Nor should there be obscenity, foolish talk or coarse joking, which are out of place, but rather thanksgiving. [5]For of this you can be sure: No immoral, impure or greedy person—such a man is an idolater—has any inheritance in the kingdom of Christ and of God. [6]Let no one deceive you with empty words, for because of such things God's wrath comes on those who are disobedient. [7]Therefore do not be partners with them.[8]For you were once darkness, but now you are light in the Lord. Live as children of light [9](for the fruit of the light consists in all goodness, righteousness and truth) [10]and find out what pleases the Lord. [11]Have nothing to do with the fruitless deeds of darkness, but rather expose them. [12]For it is shameful even to mention what the disobedient do in secret. [13]But everything exposed by the light becomes visible, [14]for it is light that makes everything visible. This is why it is said: 'Wake up, O sleeper, rise from the dead, and Christ will shine on you.' [15]Be very careful, then, how you live—not as unwise but as wise, [16]making the most of every opportunity, because the days are evil.[17]Therefore do not be foolish, but understand what the Lord's will is.[18]Do not get drunk on wine, which leads to debauchery. Instead, be filled with the Spirit" Ephesians 5:1-18.*

To be filled with the Spirit means to be completely under His control. What person who is under the control of the Holy Spirit will ever take God's name in vain or use language that does not glorify God and edify man? A Christian desires to honor and glorify God. The desire to glorify God and the defamation of His name cannot co-exist. A true Christian is God's child. What son or daughter desires to bring disgrace to his or her Father? A person who takes the Lord's name in vain using it in a slanderous, disrespectful way or uses filthy language should question his or her relationship with the Lord. Unfortunately, many are led to believe that if they are faithful (by their own standards) to their church and its traditions, they will be forgiven and granted heaven. Such Scriptures as Romans 8:28-30, however, stands in sharp contrast to such belief. They teach that he who is truly a born-again Christian is being conformed to the image of Christ.

A person who is truly a Christian has been called, justified, and glorified by God in order that he or she may be conformed to the image of Jesus Christ. An image is a likeness. One who is a Christian will think, look, act, and talk more and more like Jesus. It cannot be otherwise. God Himself brings about these changes.

John the apostle informs us that Jesus Christ was the embodiment of divine light. *"¹In the beginning was the Word, and the Word was with God, and the Word was God. [2]He was with God in the beginning. [3]Through him all things were made; without him nothing was made that has been made. [4]In him was life, and that life was the light of men. [5]The light shines in the darkness, but the darkness has not understood it"* John 1:1-4. John added in verses 9-12: *"[9]The true light that gives light to every man was coming into the world. [10]He was in the world, and though the world was made through him, the world did not recognize him. [11]He came to that which was his own, but his own did not receive him. [12]Yet to all who received him, to those who believed in his name, he gave the right to become children of born not of natural descent, nor of human decision or a husband's will, but born of God."*

Those who are spiritually re-born become children of God, children according to verse 21 of chapter 3 that will manifest the works of God. The two preceding verses, however, explain why man, left to himself, cannot work the works of God; consider: *"[19]This is the verdict: Light has come into the world, but men loved darkness instead of light because their deeds were evil. [20]Everyone who does evil hates the light, and will not come into the light for fear that his deeds will be exposed."*

The Holy Spirit regenerates each one to whom He has been sent (John 3:1-8), and that person becomes born again. According to Ephesians 4:17-5:7 his new spiritual birth will always result in the following:

"[17]So I tell you this, and insist on it in the Lord, that you must no longer live as the Gentiles do [in context: the unregenerate], in the futility of their thinking. [18]They are darkened in their understanding and separated from the life of God because of the ignorance that is in them due to the hardening of their hearts. [19]Having lost all sensitivity, they have given themselves over to sensuality so as to indulge in every kind of impurity, with a continual lust for more. [20]You, however, did not come to know Christ that way. [21]Surely you heard of him and were taught in him in accordance with the truth that is in Jesus. [22]You were taught, with regard to your former way of life, to put off your old self, which is being corrupted by its deceitful desires; [23]to be made new in the attitude of your minds; [24]and to put on the new self, created to be like God in true righteousness and holiness. [25]Therefore each of you must put off falsehood and speak truthfully to his neighbor, for we are all members of one body. [26]'In your anger do not sin' Do not let the sun go down while you are still angry, [27]and do not give the devil a foothold. [28]He who has been stealing must steal no longer, but must work, doing something useful with his own hands, that he may have something to share with those in need. [29]Do not let any unwholesome talk come out of your mouths, but only what is helpful for building

others up according to their needs, that it may benefit those who listen. [30]And do not grieve the Holy Spirit of God, with whom you were sealed for the day of redemption. [31]Get rid of all bitterness, rage and anger, brawling and slander, along with every form of malice. [32]Be kind and compassionate to one another, forgiving each other, just as in Christ God forgave you.

5:1 Be imitators of God, therefore, as dearly loved children [2]and live a life of love, just as Christ loved us and gave himself up for us as a fragrant offering and sacrifice to God. [3]But among you there must not be even a hint of sexual immorality, or of any kind of impurity, or of greed, because these are improper for God's holy people. [4]Nor should there be obscenity, foolish talk or coarse joking, which are out of place, but rather thanksgiving. [5]For of this you can be sure: No immoral, impure or greedy person—such a man is an idolater—has any inheritance in the kingdom of Christ and of God. [6]Let no one deceive you with empty words, for because of such things God's wrath comes on those who are disobedient. [7]Therefore do not be partners with them." This was Paul's admonition to the Ephesians <u>and</u> to us; what a warning!

If there has been a change in one's life, there has been a change; this is a fact of spiritual

21

rebirth. The Holy Spirit was sent by Jesus to indwell the believer as a helper, a guide, and He brings change. It must be realized, however, being indwelt does not necessarily mean a Christian is constantly under the complete control and authority of the Holy Spirit. There are times when a Christian is completely surrendered to the Holy Spirit and other times when he quenches His authority. During these times, he may slip into old habits, but there will always be consequences. The in-dwelling Holy Spirit will always convict the born-again person of sin and urge confession and repentance. How can one (such as the person mentioned at the beginning of this discourse) habitually use profanity or vulgarities without becoming uncomfortable within himself if he is truly a Christian?

Such language, habitually used or as a slip of the tongue, is not conducive with a Christian's nature. He cannot be at peace with himself or with God. If he takes the Lord's name in vain, uses profanities or vulgarities, and does not sense guilt, something is amiss in his life. Each person who is enslaved by this habit (or any other habit that is contrary to a life that reflects the Lord Jesus Christ) should take stock of himself. Am I truly born again? Am I really a Christian? Have I been deluding myself into believing that what I say or do really doesn't matter?

From the mount (Matthew 7:21-23), Jesus said: *"²¹Not everyone who says to me, 'Lord, Lord,' will enter the kingdom of heaven, but only he who does the will of my Father who is in heaven. ²²Many will say to me on that day, 'Lord, Lord, did we not prophesy in your name, and in your name drive out demons and perform many miracles?' ²³Then I will tell them plainly, 'I never knew you. Away from me, you evildoers!'"*

Remember, if there has been a change, there is a change. Each one's measurement of himself should be: If I am truly born again (have become a Christian), my life will not be controlled by my old nature but by the new nature found in Jesus Christ. However, as we shall find in the next chapter, spiritual darkness constitutes man's spiritual depravity.

CHAPTER 2

THE DEPRAVITY OF MAN

According to Webster's Dictionary, depravity is "the state of being depraved, i.e. marked by corruption or evil." Much of what man does is evil, but is man himself corrupt? Many today would say that man is not inherently evil. They believe that man is basically good, and his morality is conditioned by influences outside himself. They who hold this position believe man is a product of his environment; that if his environment were good or were to improve, he would likewise be good or improve as the given environment improves. But what does the Bible say about man's morality?

Genesis 1:26-27 declares: *"²⁶Then God said, 'Let us make man in our image, in our likeness, and let them rule over the fish of the sea and the birds of the air, over the livestock, over all the earth, and over all the creatures that move along the ground.' ²⁷So God created man in his own image, in the image of God he created him; male and female he created them."*

Created in the image of God, man certainly had a good beginning. God, who could not create anyone or anything contrary to Himself, created man in His own image. Man was created to rule over the earth that mirrored God's rule over all creation. God proclaimed that everything He created was good according to His standards. However, as we shall see from our study, man did not remain as he was created. He became something other than when he was created. He became a fallen creation. The question is: What was the extent of that fall? Was it a fall of partial depravation or a fall of complete depravation? To answer these questions, it will be helpful to consider several passages in Genesis and Romans.

Genesis 2:8-9: *"[8]Now the LORD God had planted a garden in the east, in Eden; and there he put the man he had formed. [9]And the LORD God made all kinds of trees grow out of the ground—trees that were pleasing to the eye and good for food. In the middle of the garden were the tree of life and the tree of the knowledge of good and evil."*

Genesis 2:15-17: *"[15]The LORD God took the man and put him in the Garden of Eden to work it and take care of it. [16]And the LORD God commanded the man, 'You are free to eat from any tree in the garden; [17]but you must not eat from the tree of the knowledge of good and evil, for when you eat of it you will surely die.'"*

Genesis 3:1-8: *"¹Now the serpent was more crafty than any of the wild animals the LORD God had made. He said to the woman, 'Did God really say, You must not eat from any tree in the garden?' ²The woman said to the serpent, "We may eat fruit from the trees in the garden, ³but God did say, 'You must not eat fruit from the tree that is in the middle of the garden, and you must not touch it, or you will die.' ⁴You will not surely die,' the serpent said to the woman. ⁵'For God knows that when you eat of it your eyes will be opened, and you will be like God, knowing good and evil.' ⁶When the woman saw that the fruit of the tree was good for food and pleasing to the eye, and also desirable for gaining wisdom, she took some and ate it. She also gave some to her husband, who was with her, and he ate it. ⁷Then the eyes of both of them were opened, and they realized they were naked; so they sewed fig leaves together and made coverings for themselves.*

⁸Then the man and his wife heard the sound of the LORD God as he was walking in the garden in the cool of the day, and they hid from the LORD God among the trees of the garden."

Romans 5:12: *"Therefore, just as sin entered the world through one man, and death through sin, and in this way death came to all men, because all sinned."*

From these passages we learn God implemented a prohibition, man rebelled, and the result was death. Physical death resulted from man's rebellion (disobedience), but more significantly, spiritual death. In other words, when man rebelled (was disobedient) he separated himself from the righteousness of God from which he had been created. Adam's sin necessitated that God also separate Himself from man. Fellowship no longer existed. It is important to understand that God equated this separation with death. Just as physical death separates one from all that is living, so spiritual death separates one from God. Remember Jesus' words (John 3:1-6) to Nicodemus?

"¹Now there was a man of the Pharisees named Nicodemus, a member of the Jewish ruling council. ²He came to Jesus at night and said, 'Rabbi, we know you are a teacher who has come from God. For no one could perform the miraculous signs you are doing if God were not with him.' ³In reply Jesus declared, 'I tell you the truth, no one can see the kingdom of God unless he is born again.' ⁴'How can a man be born when he is old?' Nicodemus asked. 'Surely he cannot enter a second time into his mother's womb to be born!' ⁵Jesus answered, 'I tell you the truth, no one can enter the kingdom of God unless he is born of water and the Spirit. ⁶Flesh

gives birth to flesh, but the Spirit gives birth to spirit.'"

In order for anyone to see (understand) or enter the kingdom of God, he or she must be restored to spiritual life, be born again. Paul, in his letter to the Christians at Ephesus, explains that this spiritual rebirth occurs while one is separated from God and is dead toward God. Consider: *"¹As for you, you were dead in your transgressions and sins, ²in which you used to live when you followed the ways of this world and of the ruler of the kingdom of the air, the spirit who is now at work in those who are disobedient. ³All of us also lived among them at one time, gratifying the cravings of our sinful nature and following its desires and thoughts. Like the rest, we were by nature objects of wrath. ⁴But because of his great love for us, God, who is rich in mercy, ⁵made us alive with Christ even when we were dead in transgressions—it is by grace you have been saved"* Ephesians 2:1-5.

Paul explains the reason of man's separation from God in chapter 4:18-19. *"¹⁸They are darkened in their understanding and separated from the life of God because of the ignorance that is in them due to the hardening of their hearts. ¹⁹Having lost all sensitivity, they have given themselves over to sensuality so as to indulge in every kind of impurity, with a continual lust for more."*

After reading these passages, we should have no trouble understanding how far man has been separated from a Holy God, but should there be someone still in doubt, consider Luke 16:19-31:

"19There was a rich man who was dressed in purple and fine linen and lived in luxury every day. 20At his gate was laid a beggar named Lazarus, covered with sores 21and longing to eat what fell from the rich man's table. Even the dogs came and licked his sores. 22The time came when the beggar died and the angels carried him to Abraham's side. The rich man also died and was buried. 23In hell, where he was in torment, he looked up and saw Abraham far away, with Lazarus by his side. 24So he called to him, 'Father Abraham, have pity on me and send Lazarus to dip the tip of his finger in water and cool my tongue, because I am in agony in this fire.' 25But Abraham replied, 'Son, remember that in your lifetime you received your good things, while Lazarus received bad things, but now he is comforted here and you are in agony. 26And besides all this, between us and you a great chasm has been fixed, so that those who want to go from here to you cannot, nor can anyone cross over from there to us.' 27He answered, 'Then I beg you, father, send

Lazarus to my father's house, ²⁸for I have five brothers. Let him warn them, so that they will not also come to this place of torment.' ²⁹Abraham replied, 'They have Moses and the Prophets; let them listen to them.' ³⁰'No, father Abraham, he said, but if someone from the dead goes to them, they will repent.' ³¹He said to him, 'If they do not listen to Moses and the Prophets, they will not be convinced even if someone rises from the dead.'" In these verses, Jesus taught His disciples about the separation that exists between that which is godly and that which is of the world. The world is separated from God and dead toward Him to the extent that people would not be persuaded to believe God's goodness though one should appear from the dead.

Certainly, this should answer the question about man's separation from God, but is there a way back for man? Is man able to restore himself to fellowship with God? Beyond this, **does he have a desire to do so**? In answer to these questions, we return to the beginning once again and consider Genesis 3:6-8: *"⁶When the woman saw that the fruit of the tree was good for food and pleasing to the eye, and also desirable for gaining wisdom, she took some and ate it. She also gave some to her husband, who was with her, and he ate it. ⁷Then the eyes of both of them were opened, and they realized they were naked; so* *they sewed fig leaves together and made coverings for themselves. [8]Then the man and his wife heard the sound of the LORD God as he was walking in the garden in the cool of the day, and they hid from the LORD God among the trees of the garden."*

Two things occurred in the Garden that day concerning man's fellowship (represented in Adam) with God. First, fear of God resulted from Adam's disobedience. From that time on, unregenerate man has tried to hide himself from God by one means or another. Secondly, as seen in the account of Cain and Abel, there is a denial and refusal by man (represented in Cain) to accept God's provision of forgiveness and restoration to righteousness. We read from Genesis 4:1-10 *"[1]Adam lay with his wife Eve, and she became pregnant and gave birth to Cain. She said, 'With the help of the LORD I have brought forth a man.' [2]Later she gave birth to his brother Abel. Now Abel kept flocks, and Cain worked the soil. [3]In the course of time Cain brought some of the fruits of the soil as an offering to the LORD. [4]But Abel brought fat portions from some of the firstborn of his flock. The LORD looked with favor on Abel and his offering, [5]but on Cain and his offering he did not look with favor. So Cain was very angry, and his face was downcast. [6]Then the LORD said to Cain, 'Why are you angry? Why is your face downcast? [7]If you do what is right, will you not be accepted? But if you do not do what is right, sin is crouching at your door; it desires to have you, but you must master it.' ⁸Now Cain said to his brother Abel, 'Let's go out to the field.' And while they were in the field, Cain attacked his brother Abel and killed him. ⁹Then the LORD said to Cain, 'Where is your brother Abel?' 'I don't know,' he replied. 'Am I my brother's keeper?' ¹⁰The LORD said, 'What have you done? Listen! Your brother's blood cries out to me from the ground.'"*

Before expelling Adam and Eve from the Garden, God demonstrated that He would not and could not accept man's attempt to satisfy His righteousness. We read that Adam and Eve attempted to cover their physical and spiritual nakedness with fig leaves. God, however, for reasons revealed throughout Scripture, could not accept their attempts, but instead slew an innocent animal and covered them with its hide. This was a figure of the ultimate sacrifice of Jesus Christ for man's sin. Ever since the fall, man has denied the truth of God and His provision for the atonement of sin. By offering a bloodless sacrifice, Cain refused to sacrifice an animal (a picture of the sacrifice of Jesus Christ) as commanded by God. Man, ever since, has been in denial of this same thing. He has gone about to establish his own righteousness and

33

has refused the righteousness of God. Paul writing about his own countrymen said: *"¹Brothers, my heart's desire and prayer to God for the Israelites is that they may be saved. ²For I can testify about them that they are zealous for God, but their zeal is not based on knowledge. ³Since they did not know the righteousness that comes from God and sought to establish their own, they did not submit to God's righteousness" Romans 10:1-3.*

This is not only true of Israel, but of humanity in general. Returning once again to Paul's letter to the Ephesians we read: *"¹¹Therefore, remember that formerly you who are Gentiles by birth and called 'uncircumcised' by those who call themselves 'the circumcision' (that done in the body by the hands of men)— ¹²remember that at that time you were separate from Christ, excluded from citizenship in Israel and foreigners to the covenants of the promise, without hope and without God in the world" Ephesians 2:11-12.* This depravity is traced back in time to the valley of Shinar where Nimrod led the descendants of Noah away from Holy God. We read from Genesis 11:1-9 that even though mankind had been destroyed because of their wickedness, the first generations after the flood still refused to bow the knee to God and thought to build an empire excluding His authority over them.

"¹Now the whole world had one language and a common speech. ²As men moved eastward, they found a plain in Shinar and settled there. ³They said to each other, 'Come, let's make bricks and bake them thoroughly.' They used brick instead of stone, and tar for mortar. ⁴Then they said, 'Come, let us build ourselves a city, with a tower that reaches to the heavens, so that we may make a name for ourselves and not be scattered over the face of the whole earth.' ⁵But the LORD came down to see the city and the tower that the men were building. ⁶The LORD said, 'If as one people speaking the same language they have begun to do this, then nothing they plan to do will be impossible for them. ⁷Come, let us go down and confuse their language so they will not understand each other.' ⁸So the LORD scattered them from there over all the earth, and they stopped building the city. ⁹That is why it was called Babel—because there the LORD confused the language of the whole world. From there the LORD scattered them over the face of the whole earth."

These people, in essence, sought to form their own government refusing to be ruled by God. They thought to devise their own means of reaching heaven. Man's <u>religion</u> is exposed in this passage.

Moving ahead in history, we turn to the nation of Israel. Israel descended from Abraham through Isaac and Jacob. God changed Jacob's name to Israel, and in time, Jacob fathered twelve sons. These twelve each procreated families of their own, which multiplied into tribes and became the nation of Israel. In God's plan, He chose and blessed this nation above all others and through them manifested His love, goodness, and mercy toward mankind. God promised to bless Israel beyond measure if they would worship and be obedient to Him.

The rest of the world was idolatrous toward God, creating gods of their own imaginations. They refused to recognize or worship Him as the only true God. As a testimony of His righteousness and goodness, God gave Israel a land of their own, a place flowing with milk and honey that would provide all their needs. God gave them victory over peoples who occupied this land and promised to protect them from any and all attacks. As a testimony that He indeed was the God of Israel, He gave them His love, protection, and provision, and implemented conditions by which Israel was to live. These conditions were meant as a guide so that Israel could live in righteousness before God and set them apart from the rest of mankind. The blessings that would be granted Israel, if they were obedient, was to be His testimony to all the world of His grace toward them, likewise His chastisement if they were disobedient.

Five Points:

No matter how good God was to His people, Israel as a nation would not honor or worship Him. Rather than bringing other nations to their God, they worshipped the created gods of other nations. God saw these nations as being totally depraved and He deemed those other nations so corrupt that He commanded Israel to utterly destroy many of them and gave Israel victory over others. Victory came by way of death and destruction.

When obedient, there were times when Israel experienced the blessings of God, but often they chose to be disobedient. No matter how many times God forgave them of idolatry, Israel would not remain faithful to Him. They instead turned to the gods of other nations. Again, man's depravity is shown through the nation of Israel. God eventually removed Israel as His faithful servant and chose another people through whom He would work, for a time.

During this time of being set aside Israel murdered their (and our) Redeemer. Even though God promised to reestablish His government in their midst and give them His anointed as Savior and King, they rejected Him. In rejecting Him, they abandoned God's authority and rule over them. They wanted a king and Savior of their own imaginations. They looked for a king who would re-establish them as the ruling kingdom of the earth but would not subject them to His (God's) authority. Again, man's depravity is demonstrated.

The other people, mentioned above, are the church of Jesus Christ. The church is a called-out assembly of people from all nations of earth and has been given the Holy Spirit as an indwelling help. Yet the professing church (not the possessing) has tried, and in many cases compromised, its faithfulness to Christ. In the end, it will degenerate into great apostasy - so great an apostasy that Jesus Himself is no longer inside the professed church, but according to Revelation 3:20, is outside the church asking admittance. *"Here I am! I stand at the door and knock. If anyone hears my voice and opens the door, I will come in and eat with him, and he with me."* Again, this points to the depravity of man.

Even after the calamities of the seven-year tribulation that is to come at the end of this age the unredeemed of the earth will not turn to God for mercy (Revelation 6:12-17):

[12] "I watched as he opened the sixth seal. There was a great earthquake. The sun turned black like sackcloth made of goat hair, the whole moon turned blood red, [13]and the stars in the sky fell to earth, as late figs drop from a fig tree when shaken by a strong wind. [14]The sky receded like a scroll, rolling up, and every mountain and island was removed from its place. [15]Then the kings of the earth, the princes, the generals, the rich, the mighty, and every slave and every free man hid in caves and among the rocks of the mountains. [16]They called to the mountains and the rocks, 'Fall on us and hide us from the face of him who sits on the throne and from the wrath of the Lamb! [17]For the great day of their wrath has come, and who can stand?'"

Rather than turn to the Lord Jesus Christ in repentance, begging for mercy, they attempt to hide from Him. Again, this points to the depravity of man.

After this evidence, there cannot be any doubt about man's depravity. But the question remains, "To what extent is this depravity? Is it partial, or is it total?" I think we have already answered this question, but if doubt still remains, consider the words of Jesus as recorded in John 3:19-21: *"[19]This is the verdict: Light has come into the world, but men loved darkness instead of light because their deeds were evil. [20]Everyone who does evil hates the light, and will not come into the light for fear that his deeds will be exposed. [21]But whoever lives by the truth comes into the light, so that it may be seen plainly that what he has done has been done through God."*

Jesus' declaration was that those who do evil refuse to come to the light, and He added that even those who do come to the light do so only because of what God has wrought in their lives. He declared later in John's testimony (6:44): *"No one can come to me unless the Father who sent me draws him."* And remember, Jesus said that a man must be born again in order to see or enter the kingdom of God.

"[1]Now there was a man of the Pharisees named Nicodemus, a member of the Jewish ruling council. [2]He came to Jesus at night and said, 'Rabbi, we know you are a teacher who has come from God. For no one could perform the miraculous signs you are doing if God were not with him.' [3]In reply Jesus declared, 'I tell you the truth, no one can see the kingdom of God

unless he is born again.' *⁴'How can a man be born when he is old?' Nicodemus asked. 'Surely he cannot enter a second time into his mother's womb to be born!' ⁵Jesus answered, 'I tell you the truth, no one can enter the kingdom of God unless he is born of water and the Spirit. ⁶Flesh gives birth to flesh, but the Spirit gives birth to spirit. ⁷You should not be surprised at my saying, You must be born again. ⁸The wind blows wherever it pleases. You hear its sound, but you cannot tell where it comes from or where it is going. So it is with everyone born of the Spirit'"* John 3:1-8.

Certainly, Jesus declared that in himself, man is lost. Man is not only lost and unable to save himself, but has no desire to do so unless God the Father draws him (or her) to Jesus for salvation. How could this be clearer?

"The man without the Spirit does not accept the things that come from the Spirit of God, for they are foolishness to him, and he cannot understand them, because they are spiritually discerned" 1 Corinthians 2:14.

And recalling passages already utilized, we read:

"¹As for you, you were dead in your transgressions and sins, ²in which you used to

*live when you followed the ways of this world
and of the ruler of the kingdom of the air, the
spirit who is now at work in those who are
disobedient. ³All of us also lived among them at
one time, gratifying the cravings of our sinful
nature and following its desires and thoughts.
Like the rest, we were by nature objects of
wrath. ⁴But because of his great love for us,
God, who is rich in mercy, ⁵made us alive with
Christ even when we were dead in
transgressions—it is by grace you have been
saved. ⁶And God raised us up with Christ and
seated us with him in the heavenly realms in
Christ Jesus, ⁷in order that in the coming ages
he might show the incomparable riches of his
grace, expressed in his kindness to us in Christ
Jesus. ⁸For it is by grace you have been saved,
through faith—and this not from yourselves, it
is the gift of God—⁹not by works, so that no one
can boast. ¹⁰For we are God's workmanship,
created in Christ Jesus to do good works, which
God prepared in advance for us to do"*
Ephesians 2:1-10.

*"¹¹He (Jesus) came to that which was his own,
but his own did not receive him. ¹²Yet to all who
received him, to those who believed in his name,
he gave the right to become children of God—
¹³children born not of natural descent, nor of
human decision or a husband's will, but born of
God"* John 1:11-13.

Even those whom Jesus chose to be His disciples were chosen not because of their own will, nor of their heredity or nationality, but by the will of God.

Finally, turning once again to the writings of the apostle Paul, we read: *"¹Therefore, there is now no condemnation for those who are in Christ Jesus, ²because through Christ Jesus the law of the Spirit of life set me free from the law of sin and death. ³For what the law was powerless to do in that it was weakened by the sinful nature, God did by sending his own Son in the likeness of sinful man to be a sin offering. And so he condemned sin in sinful man, ⁴in order that the righteous requirements of the law might be fully met in us, who do not live according to the sinful nature but according to the Spirit. ⁵Those who live according to the sinful nature have their minds set on what that nature desires; but those who live in accordance with the Spirit have their minds set on what the Spirit desires. ⁶The mind of sinful man is death, but the mind controlled by the Spirit is life and peace; ⁷the sinful mind is hostile to God. It does not submit to God's law, nor can it do so. ⁸Those controlled by the sinful nature cannot please God"* Romans 8:1-8.

And from Romans 8:28-30 *"²⁸And we know that in all things God works for the good of*

43

those who love him, who have been called according to his purpose. ²⁹For those God foreknew he also predestined to be conformed to the likeness of his Son, that he might be the firstborn among many brothers. ³⁰And those he predestined, he also called; those he called, he also justified; those he justified, he also glorified." This demonstrates that our salvation is totally dependant on God's mercy and grace. He has called those who are saved out of spiritual darkness and regenerated in them new spiritual life. Those who turn to God do so because of what God initiates in their lives. Without this, man is lost.

We should remember we are not here for our own benefit; God created us for His own good pleasure and to glorify Himself. He is glorified when He redeems a person, and as He conforms this person to the image of the Lord Jesus Christ. He will be glorified in the end of time when He judges the unredeemed for their sin and refusal to come to Him for forgiveness and mercy. All sin must be reconciled. It is either dealt with at the cross of Jesus or it will be dealt with at the White Throne Judgment. When one comes to the cross, he does so crying out for forgiveness and mercy. When one rejects the cross, he calls God a liar, denying that Christ's sacrifice is sufficient to satisfy God's judgment against sin.

We all are approaching the inevitable. We are all approaching the death of our bodies. This is an undeniable fact. We are going to die. One hundred per cent of people die. But what occurs after death? If God exists, and He does, we are subject to Him, not He to us. It is His world, and we will be judged by His righteous, holy standards, not our own.

Some people's bodies will not die in the normal understanding of death. They will, however, go through an instantaneous change. Please consider 1 Corinthians 15:50-54:

"[50]I declare to you, brothers, that flesh and blood cannot inherit the kingdom of God, nor does the perishable inherit the imperishable. [51]Listen, I tell you a mystery: We will not all sleep, but we will all be changed—[52]in a flash, in the twinkling of an eye, at the last trumpet. For the trumpet will sound, the dead will be raised imperishable, and we will be changed. [53]For the perishable must clothe itself with the imperishable, and the mortal with immortality. [54]When the perishable has been clothed with the imperishable, and the mortal with immortality, then the saying that is written will come true": "Death has been swallowed up in victory."

Thank you, Lord Jesus; you have taken us who have been redeemed out of spiritual darkness, placing in us your light and have removed a heart of depravity giving us a heart that seeks your holiness, and you have destined us to heaven either by resurrection or rapture.

CHAPTER 3

MAN'S WILL: FREE OR OTHERWISE?

Today, many people claim that man has a free will, a will that reaches even into heaven. This is the belief that man can choose to follow God and forsake the allurements of the world (the flesh), but is this true? Scripture affirms that man has a will, but is he free to choose God? The answers to these questions are not only interesting, but are of utmost importance.

All will agree that when making a choice, there needs to be options available. Man chooses between at least two different alternatives. Coming to a fork in a road, he will actually choose between four possibilities. He can go to the right, go to the left, return in the direction from which he came, or stay at that intersection. To get where he wants to go, he must make a decision. In making that decision, he has an objective; i.e. to go toward a desired destination, one he knows or suspects is there. Likewise, choices are available when one chooses to follow one leader or another. Whichever the scenario, choice has an intended purpose and is not without motive. Choice has a goal, a purpose, and is therefore not abstract. Choices are influenced by the want or need of the goal (or purpose) and are always made from the greater influence of the time. Man's will, therefore, is not arbitrary, but exercised toward a choice that is made according to the greatest influence at the time of decision. It cannot be any different when one makes a choice toward God or against Him. What, after all, influences man's decision to choose between God and the world? Does man in his natural state have a free will to choose toward God? Using the example above about the fork in the road, the traveler will decide from among known facts. He knows that his destination lies either to his right or left. He knows that it is not behind him, nor is it at his present location. If he has information that his destination is to the right, then he will choose to go the right. If his destination is to the left, he will choose that direction. Another option is to guess, but even this has prejudices to which he succumbs. Decision or exercise of the will, then, is subject to the greater prejudice or influence at the time of determination. It can never be otherwise.

The problem with the ability of man to choose to follow God rather than the world or his own flesh is that, according to Scripture, man in his natural state is dead toward God. Ephesians 2:1-5 states, *"[1]As for you, you were dead in your transgressions and sins, [2]in which you used to live when you followed the ways of*

48

this world and of the ruler of the kingdom of the air, the spirit who is now at work in those who are disobedient. ³All of us also lived among them at one time, gratifying the cravings of our sinful nature and following its desires and thoughts. Like the rest, we were by nature objects of wrath. ⁴But because of his great love for us, God, who is rich in mercy, ⁵made us alive with Christ even when we were dead in *transgressions—it is by grace you have been saved."* Paul explained to the Christians of Ephesus (and to us, the Christians of today), that before He made us alive in Christ, we were dead toward God.

Romans 5:12 states that *"sin entered into the world through one man (Adam) and so death came to all mankind."* This death went beyond physical; it was also spiritual. Scripture tells us (Genesis 2:17) that God warned Adam and Eve about partaking of the fruit of the Tree of the Knowledge of Good and Evil. He told them if they disobeyed, they would die. This is exactly what happened when Adam and Eve disobeyed; they died spiritually toward God. Jesus would later explain to Nicodemus (and us) that for a man to be spiritually alive again he must be born again. Consider John 3:1-8:

"¹Now there was a man of the Pharisees named Nicodemus, a member of the Jewish ruling council. ²He came to Jesus at night and said, 'Rabbi, we know you are a teacher who has come from God. For no one could perform the miraculous signs you are doing if God were not with him.' ³In reply Jesus declared, 'I tell you the truth, no one can see the kingdom of God unless he is born again'. ⁴'How can a man be born when he is old?' Nicodemus asked. 'Surely he cannot enter a second time into his mother's womb to be born!' ⁵Jesus answered, 'I tell you the truth, no one can enter the kingdom of God unless he is born of water and the Spirit. ⁶Flesh gives birth to flesh, but the Spirit gives birth to spirit. ⁷You should not be surprised at my saying, You must be born again. ⁸The wind blows wherever it pleases. You hear its sound, but you cannot tell where it comes from or where it is going. So it is with everyone born of the Spirit.'"

Paul wrote in 1 Corinthians 2:14: *"¹⁴The man without the Spirit does not accept the things that come from the Spirit of God, for they are foolishness to him, and he cannot understand them, because they are spiritually discerned."*

It is evident from these two passages that man cannot choose to follow God by an exercise of his will apart from a benevolent God. It is likewise affirmed that the things of God are seen as foolishness to the natural man.

The apostle John wrote: *"¹¹He came to that which was his own, but his own did not receive him. ¹²Yet to all who received him, to those who believed in his name, he gave the right to become children of God—¹³children born not of natural descent, nor of human decision or a husband's will, but born of God" John 1:11-13.* Those of Jesus' people (the Jews) received Him because they were born of God. Jesus said of His own disciples, *"You did not choose me, but I chose you and appointed you to go and bear fruit—fruit that will last" John 15:16a.*

Referring once again to Ephesians 2:8-10 we read: *"⁸For it is by grace you have been saved, through faith—and this not from yourselves, it is the gift of God—⁹not by works, so that no one can boast. ¹⁰For we are God's workmanship, created in Christ Jesus to do good works, which God prepared in advance for us to do."* Those who are saved (made alive toward God) are saved by the grace (unmerited favor) of God. Even the faith necessary to believe, according to verse eight, is a "gift of God." The writer of Hebrews wrote in chapter 2 verse 12 that Jesus is the author (originator) and finisher of the Christian's faith.

Some hold that man may on his own, without the efficacious influence of the Holy Spirit, choose to follow God. They use such verses as John 3:16 in support of this contention: *"God so loved the world that He gave His only begotten Son that whosoever believes in Him should not perish but have everlasting life."* However, if these individuals would read on in chapter 3 they would discover that Jesus added, *"This is the verdict: Light has come into the world, but men loved darkness instead of light because their deeds were evil"* John 3:19.

Man has a heart that is set against God (John 15:18). As a result of his nature, he will never choose or prefer the divine and spiritual apart from a new nature imparted to him by God. In other words, he must be born again. I believe the Scriptures are clear; man has a free will, but it can and always will choose that which it knows. Since man in his natural state does not know God, he will always choose that which he *does* know, the way of his flesh and the way of the world.

For those readers who have been redeemed, consider your own salvation. Was there not a time when you were unwilling to come to Christ? Since you have come to Him, are you prepared to give Him all the glory and join with the writer of Psalm 115:1 and sing out:

"Not to us, O Lord, not to us but to your name be the glory because of your love and faithfulness." The Christian must acknowledge he or she came to Christ because the Holy Spirit brought them from unwillingness to willingness.

For those who have not been redeemed (born again), please realize that if you are being drawn to God, it is by His volition, not yours. If you truly are seeking God, it is because He has called you. He will not turn you away. If you are being drawn to God, **you will** come and commit to Him. Romans 8:28-30 declares God's finished product: *"[28]And we know that in all things God works for the good of those who love him, who have been called according to his purpose. [29]For those God foreknew he also predestined to be conformed to the likeness of his Son, that he might be the firstborn among many brothers. [30]And those he predestined, he also called; those he called, he also justified; those he justified, he also glorified."*

God calls out from humanity those who become redeemed, not in response to their will, but according to His will. He calls them not because they have chosen Him, but because He has chosen them. He lightens their path through the illumination of the Holy Spirit so they may see their need of spiritual renewal.

For any sinner to be saved, three things are indispensable: God the Father must purpose his salvation (and He has), God the Son must purchase his salvation (and He has), and the God Holy Spirit must bring it to pass (and He has). Man's salvation is exclusively the work of God, and this work was concluded before the creation of the world. Revelation 13:8 tells us that the Lamb of God was slain from the foundation of the creation in order that those whose names are written in the His "Book of Life" (Revelation 17:8) could be redeemed.

We note, Romans 8:28-30 declares man's calling, justification, and glorification is the work of God, and Revelation 17:8 declares that the names of those who were to be redeemed were written in the "Book of Life" in eternity past, before creation. Nowhere in either passage is man's choice or efforts mentioned.

Some might wonder if this is all true. Why do people around the world worship their concept of God and yet are not born again? In answer, it must be remembered: When man sinned (represented in Adam), he did not then become a creation without a spirit (soul). Although he died in the spiritual sense toward God, man was still a spiritual being retaining a desire to worship an entity outside of himself. In demonstration of this truth we read from Romans 1:18-23 the mindset of the Gentile peoples during the years that God reached out to mankind through the children of Israel.

"[18]The wrath of God is being revealed from heaven against all the godlessness and wickedness of men who suppress the truth by their wickedness, [19]since what may be known about God is plain to them, because God has made it plain to them. [20]For since the creation of the world God's invisible qualities—his eternal power and divine nature—have been clearly seen, being understood from what has been made, so that men are without excuse. [21]For although they knew God, they neither glorified him as God nor gave thanks to him, but their thinking became futile and their foolish hearts were darkened. [22]Although they claimed to be wise, they became fools [23]and exchanged the glory of the immortal God for images made to look like mortal man and birds and animals and reptiles." This mindset, of course, transcends the Gentiles of that time to all peoples whom have not yet been redeemed. All persons before redemption worship their concept of God, the god of their own imaginations.

Romans 3:10-12 states: *"¹⁰As it is written: 'There is no one righteous, not even one; ¹¹there is no one who understands, no one who seeks God. ¹²All have turned away, they have together become worthless; there is no one who does good, not even one.'"*

God calls fallen man out of spiritual darkness, regenerates the inner man to God consciousness, and creates within man a new desire of fellowship with Him. Then, and only then, does man call out to God. In the process, God provides the message, the messenger, and the Holy Spirit. The Holy Spirit regenerates, illuminates, convicts, and converts. Consider Romans 10:13-15 and I Corinthians 1:18-25:

Romans 10:13: *"For whosoever shall call upon the name of the Lord shall be saved. ¹⁴How then shall they call on him in whom they have not believed? and how shall they believe in him of whom they have not heard? and how shall they hear without a preacher? ¹⁵And how shall they preach, except they be sent? as it is written, 'How beautiful are the feet of them that preach the gospel of peace, and bring glad tidings of good things!'"*

First Corinthians 1:18: *"For the preaching of the cross is to them that perish foolishness; but unto us which are saved it is the power of God. ¹⁹For it is written, 'I will destroy the wisdom of the wise, and will bring to nothing the understanding of the prudent.' [20]Where is the wise? where is the scribe? Where is the disputer of this world? hath not God made foolish the wisdom of this world? [21]For after that in the wisdom of God the world by wisdom knew not God, it pleased God by the foolishness of preaching to save them that believe. [22]For the Jews require a sign, and the Greeks seek after wisdom: [23]But we preach Christ crucified, unto the Jews a stumbling block, and unto the Greeks foolishness; [24]But unto them, which are called, both Jews and Greeks, Christ the power of God, and the wisdom of God. [25]Because the foolishness of God is wiser than men; and the weakness of God is stronger than men."*

In summary, God has purposed to save man by and through His Word. He has called certain ones to salvation and accomplishes this at His determined time. Someone might ask, "If salvation is not by the choice (free will) of man but by the calling of God, why are we to go around the world testifying of His grace and calling people to repentance?" The answer is this; we don't know who are to be saved. Only God knows and brings it about through His Word and the regenerating work of the Holy Spirit. Believers are to go forth giving out the good news found in Jesus Christ. As the Christian shares the good news of Christ's sacrifice on behalf of those called,

57

the Holy Spirit brings conviction and conversion. In my mind (and I think this is the fact of Scripture), God grants new life to those of His sovereign calling. He, through the work of the Holy Spirit, opens their understanding, creates in them an awareness of Himself and causes a repentant heart, a commitment to Himself, and a desire of fellowship. He reverses the consequence of sin that had separated man from God.

If we understand this, we have come to an appreciation of God's grace. Furthermore, we are prompted to engage in a spirit of worship and are inspired toward practical godliness and zeal in service. This appreciation of God's grace should comfort our hearts, strengthen our souls, and bless our lives. On the other hand, if we hold to the belief that we chose to come to God on our own, we diminish in our thinking the gift of Christ's sacrificial death and the need for the intervention of the Holy Spirit to call us out of spiritual darkness.

CHAPTER 4

THE FALLACY OF AN EASY SALVATION

In his book, A Laymen's Guide to the Lordship Controversy, Richard P. Belcher writes,

> If one were to suggest that the time would come when a group of evangelical Christians would be arguing for a salvation without repentance, without a change of behavior or lifestyle, without a real avowal of the lordship and authority of Christ, without perseverance, without discipleship, and a salvation which does not necessarily result in obedience and works, and with a regeneration which does not necessarily change one's life, most believers of several decades ago would have felt such would be an absolute impossibility. But believe it or not, the hour has come.

If what Mr. Belcher writes is true, and I believe it is, then how should we evangelize our friends, our family, and neighbors? How should we present the gospel to our children? Certainly we should not present a deluded gospel, yet Christians today are often cautioned not to say too much to the lost.

Certain spiritual issues are labeled taboo when speaking to the unconverted: God's law, Christ's lordship, repentance, surrender, obedience, judgment, and hell are not to be mentioned, lest we add something to the offer of God's free gift. Many evangelicals have come to wrongly apply the doctrine of "faith alone." They make faith the only permissible topic when speaking to non-Christians about a personal relationship with Jesus Christ, believing that this preserves the purity of the gospel. What this has done is weaken the message of salvation. It has also populated the church with "converts" whose faith is counterfeit and whose hope hangs on a bogus or false promise. These people say they "accept Christ as Savior," yet brazenly reject His rightful claim as Lord. They pay lip service, but utterly scorn Him with their hearts (Mark 7:6). They casually affirm Him with their mouths, although they deliberately deny Him with their deeds (Titus 1:16). They address Him superficially as "Lord, Lord," yet stubbornly decline to do His bidding (Luke 6:46). Such people fit the tragic description of the "many" in Matthew 7:23 who will one day be stunned to hear Him (Jesus) say, *I never knew you; depart from Me, you who practice lawlessness.*

The fallacy of one choosing Jesus Christ as Savior is a prevalent belief today in evangelism. Truly, one does choose Christ as Savior, but this follows the work of the Holy Spirit. Many of the evangelical persuasion have come to believe, however, that choosing Christ originates within man and then the Holy Spirit comes alongside to aid the one making the decision. A "decision for Christ" is usually signified by some physical or verbal act such as raising a hand, walking an aisle, repeating a prayer, signing a card, reciting a pledge, or something similar. If the sinner performs the prescribed activity, the "moment of decision" becomes the ground of the person's assurance. Scripture refutes these fallacies:

John 3:3-6 states: *"[3]In reply Jesus answered and said unto him, Verily, verily, I say unto thee, Except a man be born again, he cannot see the kingdom of God. [4]Nicodemus saith unto him, How can a man be born when he is old? can he enter the second time into his mother's womb, and be born? [5]Jesus answered, Verily, verily, I say unto thee, Except a man be born of water and of the Spirit, he cannot enter into the kingdom of God. [6]That which is born of the flesh is flesh; and that which is born of the Spirit is spirit."(KJV)*

Ephesians 2:1 says: *"And you hath he quickened, who were dead in trespasses and sins;"*

From these two passages it is clear that any movement toward God comes after the granting of newness of spiritual life. The chicken came before the egg, and life comes before faith. It is impossible for one who is dead either physically or spiritually to produce anything. Life in both cases must exist. Spiritual life produces faith and according to Ephesians 2:8 is God's gift: *"For by grace are ye saved through faith; and that not of yourselves: it is the gift of God."*

The "and that" of verse 8 refers back to the entire previous statement of salvation (2:1-7). Salvation is by grace through faith. Because it is impossible for man to believe on his own (1 Corinthians 2:9-14) faith must be initiated by God. Man comes to a point of placing faith in God, but it is not of himself. Verses 9 and 10 of Ephesians 2 affirm this truth. Consider! *"⁹Not of works, lest any man should boast. 10For we are God's workmanship, created in Christ Jesus unto good works, which God hath before ordained that we should walk in them."* If faith is of one's own device, it must be qualified as a work.

Verses 8 through 10 state clearly that faith is the work and gift of God. Salvation is more than just simply declaring, "I believe." When newness of life (spiritual awakening) occurs in a person's life, repentance also takes place. This cannot be otherwise because it is the result of the Holy Spirit softening man's heart toward God. Jesus Himself preached, *"Repent ye, and believe in the gospel" (Mark 1:15).* To believe in biblical terms always goes beyond a mere acceptance of facts. Belief points to a commitment or obligation to the object of faith, in this case the gospel, more pointedly, as in the case of salvation, to Jesus Christ. A good example of this truth is the Philippian jailer. He and his family were moved to the point of commitment to Christ, a commitment that came with a cost.

The writer of Hebrews said that Christ *"became the author of eternal salvation unto all that obey Him" Hebrews 5:9.* He was the originator of our salvation.

Paul wrote, *"That if you confess with your mouth, 'Jesus is Lord,' and believe in your heart that God raised him from the dead, you will be saved" Romans 10:9.*

Confession is a part of repentance. One must be in agreement with God about his or her sin. Confession and repentance are both components of this agreement. Even though they are different, they are not mutually exclusive of one another. They must both exist. At Pentecost, Peter preached, *"Repent, and be baptized everyone of you in the name of Jesus Christ for the remissions of sins; and you shall receive the gift of the Holy Spirit"* Acts 2:38.

There are a multitude of other Scriptures that declare that true salvation is always accompanied with repentance and being defined as, "the turning from sin to Christ." For instance, 1John 2:3-4 says: *"[3]We know that we have come to know him if we obey his commands. [4] The man who says, 'I know him,' but does not do what he commands is a liar, and the truth is not in him."*

Are we to believe that the inspired Scripture constitutes poorly worded theology? It should be obvious that Jesus and the apostles certainly held that repentance was a part of salvation. Why should we separate the two if God's Word does not? If Scripture cautioned against preaching repentance, obedience, righteousness, or judgment to unbelievers, then perhaps we would have a just cause to limit our presentation of Christ to a mental acceptance of Him. Scripture, however, contains no such warnings. The opposite is true. If we want to follow the biblical model, we cannot ignore those issues. Sin, repentance, righteousness, and judgment are the very matters about which the Holy Spirit convicts the unsaved. Can we omit them from the message and still call it the gospel? Apostolic evangelism inevitably culminated in a call for repentance (Acts 2:38; 3:19; 17:30; 26:20).

Are we to do less than they, simply telling the sinner he must "accept Christ" and not declare his need of repentance or turning from sin? Finally, to declare that by accepting Christ as Savior either by the raising of a hand, walking an aisle, or verbally accenting to that acceptance, while not declaring the necessity of repentance, is in direct contradiction of Ephesians 2:10, which states: *"For we are His workmanship created in Christ Jesus unto good works, which God hath before ordained that we should walk in them."*

God's work in the Christian begins immediately upon regeneration, conforming him or her to the image of Christ. The Holy Spirit uniquely prepares the heart of the recipient of salvation. The Holy Spirit sheds light on man's sin. The Holy Spirit calls one out of spiritual darkness. The Holy Spirit regenerates man to spiritual life. The Holy Spirit begins to conform one to the image of Jesus Christ at the point of regeneration. To put it bluntly, if there is no change in the one who claims to have accepted Christ as Savior, he or she is still in sin. May this not be true of you or me. Let us be found of the Lord as being faithful servants, such as those of Matthew 25:14-30: The Kingdom of Heaven will be *"[14]like a man going on a journey, who called his servants and entrusted his property to them. [15]To one he gave five talents of money, to another two talents of money, and to another one talent, each according to his ability. Then he went on his journey. [16] The man who had received the five talents went at once and put his money to work and gained five more. [17]So also, the one with the two talents gained two more. [18]But the man who had received the one talent went off, dug a hole in the ground and hid his master's money.[19] After a long time the master of those servants returned and settled accounts with them. [20]The man who had received the five talents brought the other five. Master, he said, you entrusted me with five talents. See, I have gained five more. [21] His master replied, Well done, good and faithful servant! You have been faithful with a few things; I will put you in charge of many things. Come and share your master's happiness! [22] The man with two talents also came, Master, he said, you entrusted me with two talents, see, I have gained two more. [23] His master replied, well done, good and faithful servant! You have been faithful with a few things; I will put you in charge of many things. Come and share your master's happiness!* ²⁴ *Then the man who had received the one talent came. Master, he said, I knew that you are a hard man, harvesting where you have not sown and gathered where you have not scattered seed.* ²⁵ *So I was afraid and went out and hid your talent in the ground. See, here is what belongs to you.* ²⁶*His master replied, you wicked, lazy servant! So you knew that I harvest where I have not sown and gather where I have not scattered seed?* ²⁷ *Well then, you should have put my money on deposit with the bankers, so that when I returned I would have received it back with interest.* ²⁸ *Take the talent from him and give it to the one who has the ten talents.* ²⁹ *For everyone who has will be given more, and he will have an abundance. Whosoever does not have, even what he has will be taken from him.* ³⁰ *And throw that worthless servant outside, into the darkness, where there will be weeping and gnashing of teeth."*

Salvation is a free gift, but it is not a free ride.

CHAPTER 5

FAITH: CHOICE OR GIFT

What is faith? Is it appropriated or is it bestowed? Webster's Dictionary describes faith as trust, having confidence. The Bible states in Hebrews 11:1: *"Now faith is the substance of things hoped for, the evidence of things not seen."* In the remainder of the chapter, the writer gives examples of how said faith played out in the lives of many Old Testament people. Consider:

"2For by it the elders obtained a good report. 3Through faith we understand that the worlds were framed by the word of God, so that things which are seen were not made of things which do appear.

4By faith Abel offered unto God a more excellent sacrifice than Cain, by which he obtained witness that he was righteous, God testifying of his gifts: and by it he being dead yet spoke.

5By faith Enoch was translated that he should not see death; and was not found, because God had translated him: for before his translation he had this testimony, that he pleased God. 6But without faith it is impossible to please him: for he that cometh to God must believe that he is, and that he is a rewarder of them that diligently seek him.

69

[7]By faith Noah, being warned of God of things not seen as yet, moved with fear, prepared an ark to the saving of his house; by the which he condemned the world, and became heir of the righteousness which is by faith.

[8]By faith Abraham, when he was called to go out into a place, which he should after receive for an inheritance, obeyed; and he went out, not knowing whither he went. [9]By faith he sojourned in the land of promise, as in a strange country, dwelling in tabernacles with Isaac and Jacob, the heirs with him of the same promise: [10]For he looked for a city which hath foundations, whose builder and maker is God.

[11]Through faith also Sarah herself received strength to conceive seed, and was delivered of a child when she was past age, because she judged him faithful who had promised. [12]Therefore sprang there even of one, and him as good as dead, so many as the stars of the sky in multitude, and as the sand which is by the sea shore innumerable.

[13]These all died in faith, not having received the promises, but having seen them afar off, and were persuaded of them, and embraced them, and confessed that they were strangers and pilgrims on the earth. [14]For they that say such things declare plainly that they seek a country. [15]And truly, if they had been mindful of that country from whence they came out, they might have had opportunity to have returned. [16]But

now they desire a better country, that is, an heavenly: wherefore God is not ashamed to be called their God: for he hath prepared for them a city.

[17] By faith Abraham, when he was tried, offered up Isaac: and he that had received the promises offered up his only begotten son, [18] Of whom it was said, That in Isaac shall thy seed be called: [19] Accounting that God was able to raise him up, even from the dead; from whence also he received him in a figure.

[20] By faith Isaac blessed Jacob and Esau concerning things to come.

[21] By faith Jacob, when he was dying, blessed both the sons of Joseph; and worshipped, leaning upon the top of his staff.

[22] By faith Joseph, when he died, made mention of the departing of the children of Israel; and gave commandment concerning his bones.

[23] By faith Moses, when he was born, was hid three months of his parents, because they saw he was a proper child; and they were not afraid of the king's commandment. [24] By faith Moses, when he was come to years, refused to be called the son of Pharaoh's daughter; [25] Choosing rather to suffer affliction with the people of God, than to enjoy the pleasures of sin for a season; [26] Esteeming the reproach of Christ greater riches than the treasures in Egypt: for he had respect unto the recompense of the reward. [27] By faith he forsook Egypt, not fearing the wrath of the king: for he endured, as seeing

him who is invisible. ²⁸Through faith he kept the Passover, and the sprinkling of blood, lest he that destroyed the firstborn should touch them. ²⁹By faith they passed through the Red sea as by dry land: which the Egyptians assaying to do were drowned.

³⁰By faith the walls of Jericho fell down, after they were compassed about seven days.

³¹By faith the harlot Rahab perished not with them that believed not, when she had received the spies with peace.

³²And what shall I more say? for the time would fail me to tell of Gideon, and of Barak, and of Samson, and of Jephthae; of David also, and Samuel, and of the prophets: ³³Who through faith subdued kingdoms, wrought righteousness, obtained promises, stopped the mouths of lions, ³⁴Quenched the violence of fire, escaped the edge of the sword, out of weakness were made strong, waxed valiant in fight, turned to flight the armies of the aliens. 35Women received their dead raised to life again: and others were tortured, not accepting deliverance; that they might obtain a better resurrection: ³⁶And others had trial of cruel mockings and scourgings, yea, moreover of bonds and imprisonment: ³⁷They were stoned, they were sawn asunder, were tempted, were slain with the sword: they wandered about in sheepskins and goatskins; being destitute, afflicted, tormented; ³⁸(Of whom the world was not worthy:) they wandered in deserts, and in mountains, and in dens and caves of the earth. ³⁹And these all,

having obtained a good report through faith, received not the promise: [40]*God having provided some better thing for us, that they without us should not be made perfect."*

In these verses, spiritual faith is defined as believing God even though He was not seen by those who believed. How was this possible for them? How is it possible for those of us in this generation? How can one believe (have confidence, i.e., trust) in the unseen God when our physical senses cry out for what can be proven only by what we see? According to the Apostle Paul, **it is not possible** for human beings in their natural state to possess faith in the unseen God. Consider his words to the Corinthian church (I Corinthians 2.14): *"The man without the Spirit does not accept the things that come from the Spirit of God, for they are foolishness to him, and he cannot understand them, because they are spiritually discerned."* The term "natural man" refers to the person who has not been born again or spiritually regenerated. For one to believe what God says, one must be transformed in his or her spirit. One must be transformed from the state of spiritual death and transformed into the state of spiritual vibrancy. Because of sin, all persons are born spiritually dead toward God and must have a spiritual renewal. Jesus said to Nicodemus in John 3:

3:3 *"I tell you the truth, no one can see the kingdom of God unless he is born again."*

3:5 *"I tell you the truth, no one can enter the kingdom of God unless he is born of water and the Spirit."*

According to these two verses, without a spiritual rebirth, no one can see (understand) (or) enter into the Kingdom of God. It follows that if one cannot understand (see) the spiritual kingdom, one cannot have faith in God. Faith in God and spiritual discernment are birthed in those who are regenerated unto new spiritual life. The context in which these two verses are found give added insight:

"[1]Now there was a man of the Pharisees named Nicodemus, a member of the Jewish ruling council. [2]He came to Jesus at night and said, 'Rabbi, we know you are a teacher who has come from God. For no one could perform the miraculous signs you are doing if God were not with him.' [3]In reply Jesus declared, 'I tell you the truth, no one can see the kingdom of God unless he is born again.' [4]'How can a man be born when he is old?' Nicodemus asked. 'Surely he cannot enter a second time into his mother's womb to be born!' [5]Jesus answered, 'I tell you the truth, no one can enter the kingdom of God unless he is born of water and the Spirit. [6]Flesh gives birth to flesh, but the Spirit gives birth to

74

spirit. ⁷You should not be surprised at my saying, You must be born again. ⁸The wind blows wherever it pleases. You hear its sound, but you cannot tell where it comes from or where it is going. So it is with everyone born of the Spirit.'" John 3.1-8.

The first prerequisite to faith, then, is being spiritually alive. Secondly, spiritual faith is not something that one may conjure up or appropriate within him or herself. According to Ephesians 2:8-10: faith is a gift of God. *"⁸For it is by grace you have been saved, through faith—and this not from yourselves, it is the gift of God—⁹not by works, so that no one can boast. ¹⁰For we are God's workmanship, created in Christ Jesus to do good works, which God prepared in advance for us to do."*

Verse eight identifies faith as the gift of God. Verse ten identifies that we are God's workmanship, created in Christ Jesus unto good works. Faith, therefore, is not an act of the will as some hold, but is a gift from sovereign God. John 1:11-13 and Romans 8:28-30 affirm this truth.

John 1:11-13: *"¹¹He came to that which was his own, but his own did not receive him. ¹²Yet to all who received him, to those who believed in his name, he gave the right to become children of God—[13]children born not of natural descent, nor of human decision or a husband's will, but born of God."*

Romans 8:28-30: " *[28]And we know that in all things God works for the good of those who love him, who have been called according to his purpose. [29]For those God foreknew he also predestined to be conformed to the likeness of his Son, that he might be the firstborn among many brothers. [30]And those he predestined, he also called; those he called, he also justified; those he justified, he also glorified."* God calls, justifies, sanctifies, and glorifies all those He calls by and through His will, not in response to man's will.

Spiritual faith cannot be experienced by the natural man but is a gift of God to those whom He redeems and regenerates. On one hand, God grants the ability to believe (to have faith). On the other hand, He works on behalf of the ones who are to receive faith in order to bring it about. He conveys the truth of His being and then overcomes spiritual darkness.

In the Old Testament, He often sent "the angel of the Lord" (deity in the flesh, a Theophany of the pre-incarnate Christ) to convey His message. At times, God spoke directly to certain ones as a voice from heaven. On many occasions He sent an angel or spoke through a prophet. In New Testament times He has spoken to us through the Lord Jesus Christ. as Hebrews 1:1-2 informs us: *"[1]In the past God spoke to our forefathers through the prophets at many times and in various ways, [2]but in these last days he has spoken to us by his Son, whom he appointed heir of all things, and through whom he made the universe."* In turn Christ empowered His followers (the apostles and certain disciples) to speak forth His word. This empowerment has passed from them to every person who becomes saved, each one in his or her own time. Hebrews 4:12 informs us of what His word is able to accomplish when delivered in the authority (the power) of the Holy Spirit. *"The word of God is living and active. Sharper than any double-edged sword, it penetrates even to dividing soul and spirit, joints and marrow; it judges the thoughts and attitudes of the heart."* It brings conviction, repentance and conversion.

In summary, saving faith is a gift, not an exercise of the will. It is brought about by the energizing power of the Holy Spirit who utilizes that which has been written or spoken about God and His Anointed One, the Lord Jesus Christ. For those who might claim that God isn't fair because He has measured faith to some and not to others, consider Romans

1:18-32: *"[18]The wrath of God is being revealed from heaven against all the godlessness and wickedness of men who suppress the truth by their wickedness, [19]since what may be known about God is plain to them, because God has made it plain to them. [20]For since the creation of the world God's invisible qualities—his eternal power and divine nature—have been clearly seen, being understood from what has been made, so that men are without excuse. [21]For although they knew God, they neither glorified him as God nor gave thanks to him, but their thinking became futile and their foolish hearts were darkened. [22]Although they claimed to be wise, they became fools [23]and exchanged the glory of the immortal God for images made to look like mortal man and birds and animals and reptiles. [24]Therefore God gave them over in the sinful desires of their hearts to sexual impurity for the degrading of their bodies with one another. [25]They exchanged the truth of God for a lie, and worshiped and served created things rather than the Creator—who is forever praised. Amen. [26]Because of this, God gave them over to shameful lusts. Even their women exchanged natural relations for unnatural ones. [27]In the same way the men also abandoned natural relations with women and were inflamed with lust for one another. Men committed indecent acts with other men, and received in themselves the due penalty for their perversion. [28]Furthermore, since they did not think it worthwhile to retain the knowledge of*

God, he gave them over to a depraved mind, to do what ought not to be done. [29]They have become filled with every kind of wickedness, evil, greed and depravity. They are full of envy, murder, strife, deceit and malice. They are gossips, [30]slanderers, God-haters, insolent, arrogant and boastful; they invent ways of doing evil; they disobey their parents; [31]they are senseless, faithless, heartless, ruthless. [32]Although they know God's righteous decree that those who do such things deserve death, they not only continue to do these very things but also approve of those who practice them."

Granted, in context, Paul is referring to the non-Israelite during the time that God had called and used the children of Israel as His witnesses to humanity, but this is applicable to all persons before regeneration, past, present, and future. Man is man and does not change on his own. The soul of man is always concerned with that which he knows. In the case of the unregenerate man, he only knows the things of the flesh. His spirit, which gives him God-consciousness, has been cut off from God. Man's spirit is dead toward God. Way back in Genesis God declared that because of sin man became separated from Him, separated to the point of death. Consider Genesis 2:17: *"...but you must not eat from the tree of the knowledge of good and evil, for when you eat of it you will surely die."*

As physical death separates one from all that is living, spiritual death separates one from God. This is affirmed by the fact that if one is to see (understand) the kingdom of God and be reunited with Him, he or she must be born again. Is God fair in exercise of His sovereignty, bestowing faith to some and not others? Those who would hold that God is not fair must deal with John 16:6-11, which states: *"6Because I have said these things, you are filled with grief. 7But I tell you the truth: It is for your good that I am going away. Unless I go away, the Counselor will not come to you; but if I go, I will send him to you. 8When he comes, he will convict the world of guilt in regard to sin and righteousness and judgment: 9in regard to sin, because men do not believe in me; 10in regard to righteousness, because I am going to the Father, where you can see me no longer; 11and in regard to judgment, because the prince of this world now stands condemned."*

The Holy Spirit has been given to convict all men of their sin, not only those to whom mercy is shown. All men deserve the wages they have earned, eternal separation from God, but He (God) said: *"I will have mercy on whom I will have mercy"* Romans 3:23a. Note the Context in which Paul proffered these words:

¹⁴"What then shall we say? Is God unjust? Not at all! ¹⁵For he says to Moses, 'I will have mercy on whom I have mercy, and I will have compassion on whom I have compassion.' ¹⁶It does not, therefore, depend on man's desire or effort, but on God's mercy. ¹⁷For the Scripture says to Pharaoh: 'I raised you up for this very purpose, that I might display my power in you and that my name might be proclaimed in all the earth. ¹⁸Therefore God has mercy on whom he wants to have mercy, and he hardens whom he wants to harden. ¹⁹One of you will say to me: 'Then why does God still blame us? For who resists his will?' ²⁰But who are you, O man, to talk back to God? Shall what is formed say to him who formed it, 'Why did you make me like this?' ²¹Does not the potter have the right to make out of the same lump of clay some pottery for noble purposes and some for common use? ²²What if God, choosing to show his wrath and make his power known, bore with great patience the objects of his wrath—prepared for destruction? ²³What if he did this to make the riches of his glory known to the objects of his mercy, whom he prepared in advance for glory—²⁴even us, whom he also called, not only from the Jews but also from the Gentiles? ²⁵As he says in Hosea: 'I will call them my people who are not my people; and I will call her my loved one who is not my loved one,' ²⁶and, 'It will happen that in the very place where it was said to them, You are not my people, they will be called sons of the living God'. ²⁷Isaiah cries *out concerning Israel: 'Though the number of the Israelites be like the sand by the sea, only the remnant will be saved. ^{28}For the Lord will carry out his sentence on earth with speed and finality'" Romans 9:14-28.*

One must remember John 3:16-18 which states: *"^{16}For God so loved the world that he gave his one and only Son, that whoever believes in him shall not perish but have eternal life. ^{17}For God did not send his Son into the world to condemn the world, but to save the world through him. ^{18}Whoever believes in him is not condemned, but whoever does not believe stands condemned already because he has not believed in the name of God's one and only Son."*

Christ's blood was shed to pay the penalty of sin; something man could not do, even if he wanted to. But because man could not and would not come on his own to God for mercy, God reached out to man in Old Testament times by giving prophets to Israel and reached through Israel to the Gentiles. In these New Testament times, He has demonstrated His love to the world by giving us His Son, the Holy Spirit, His Word, and the Church. All these are a testimony of His grace. Still, after all this, man on his own will not turn to God. Therefore, it pleased God to extend unmerited favor to those whom are to be saved, who are to be called. Man, according to Scripture, is totally depraved. That is, man in his natural state has no inclination toward the one true God. He, in essence, is spiritually dead. Remember, Jesus explained to Nicodemus (and us) in John 3:19-21: *"[19]This is the verdict: Light has come into the world, but men loved darkness instead of light because their deeds were evil. [20]Everyone who does evil hates the light, and will not come into the light for fear that his deeds will be exposed. [21]But whoever lives by the truth comes into the light, so that it may be seen plainly that what he has done has been done through God."*

Without the mercy (unmerited favor) of God, no one would have faith or salvation, but thanks to His mercy and grace, we who are His, have both.

CHAPTER 6

GRACE OR WORKS

Grace according to the Bible is the unmerited favor of God. Works on the one hand are defined as any activity that is done in an attempt to earn salvation or the favor of God; acting to appease God's wrath. On the other hand works can be defined as any activity done to honor God through the indwelling Holy Spirit.

Is man saved by grace, by works, or a combination of both? Many believe God is sovereign over everything, but add that He cannot save man unless man allows Him to do so. To do otherwise would violate man's (so-called) free will. Some say salvation is by grace (the unmerited favor of God) yet contradict this statement by saying man must do this or that to be saved, but is either of these the message of the Bible?

Before looking into Scripture to see what it says about man's salvation, it should be understood that the Bible stands alone. It's own claim is that it is the Word of God. The apostle John said emphatically: *"[18]I warn everyone who hears the words of the prophecy of this book: If anyone adds anything to them, God will add to him the plagues described in this book. [19]And if anyone takes words away from this book of prophecy, God will take away from him his share in the tree of life and in the holy city, which are described in this book."* Revelation 22.18-19.

Some question what John meant by "the prophecy of this Book." Did he mean the entire Bible or the singular "Book of the Revelation?" The question is mute, because John also wrote the gospel of John and the three epistles of 1 John, 2 John, and 3 John. All these books complement one another. Nowhere in these five books does John contradict himself. And Paul, in his second letter to Timothy, wrote: *"All Scripture is God-breathed and is useful for teaching, rebuking, correcting and training in righteousness"* 2 Timothy 3.16.

And Peter wrote in 2 Peter 1:12-21...

"[12]So I will always remind you of these things, even though you know them and are firmly established in the truth you now have. [13] I think it is right to refresh your memory as long as I live in the tent of this body, [14]because I know that I will soon put it aside, as our Lord Jesus Christ has made clear to me. [15]And I will make every effort to see that after my departure you will always be able to remember these things.

[16]We did not follow cleverly invented stories when we told you about the power and coming of our Lord Jesus Christ, but we were eyewitnesses of his majesty. [17]For he received honor and glory from God the Father when the voice came to him from the Majestic Glory, saying, 'This is my Son, whom I love; with him I am well pleased.' [18]We ourselves heard this voice that came from heaven when we were with him on the sacred mountain. [19]And we have the word of the prophets made more certain, and you will do well to pay attention to it, as to a light shining in a dark place, until the day dawns and the morning star rises in your hearts. [20]Above all, you must understand that no prophecy of Scripture came about by the prophet's own interpretation. [21]For prophecy never had its origin in the will of man, but men spoke from God as they were carried along by the Holy Spirit."

Peter's testimony was that the Word of God came by holy men of God as they were inspired and moved by the Holy Spirit. The canon of Scripture (66 books) was completed in the first century. Some tried to add certain writings after the close of that century but there were falsehoods and contradictions in their writings and these writings were not accepted. God preserved **His** Word. There are no falsehoods or contradictions within its pages. It must be understood and accepted that all other writings are an addition to those original sixty-six books. Such additions or deletions according to John will bring God's wrath upon those who do. So then, in that the Bible is God's message to man, what does the Bible say about His grace? What does it say about man's works? For an answer we begin with Ephesians 2:1-10:

"¹As for you, you were dead in your transgressions and sins, ²in which you used to live when you followed the ways of this world and of the ruler of the kingdom of the air, the spirit who is now at work in those who are disobedient. ³All of us also lived among them at one time, gratifying the cravings of our sinful nature and following its desires and thoughts. Like the rest, we were by nature objects of wrath. ⁴But because of his great love for us, God, who is rich in mercy, ⁵made us alive with Christ even when we were dead in transgressions—it is by grace you have been saved. ⁶And God raised us up with Christ and seated us with him in the heavenly realms in Christ Jesus, ⁷in order that in the coming ages he might show the incomparable riches of his grace, expressed in his kindness to us in Christ Jesus. ⁸For it is by grace you have been saved, through faith—and this not from yourselves, it is the gift of God—⁹not by works, so that no one can boast. ¹⁰For we are God's workmanship,

created in Christ Jesus to do good works, which God prepared in advance for us to do."

In verse one Paul writes that the Ephesians (you and I also) "were dead in trespasses and sins" before regeneration. That is, before being renewed spiritually toward God. Paul further explains in verses two and three that *"we were by nature objects of wrath."* This means that we were at enmity (at war) with God as we "gratified the cravings of our sinful nature." No "good" works could come out of a being such as this. To believe anything else is a denial of the truth. But even while we were in this condition, *"God, who is rich in mercy, made us alive with Christ even when we were dead in transgressions—it is by grace you (we) have been saved" Ephesians 2:4-5.*

Our regeneration, was accomplished by God and God alone. We were dead toward Him at the time of our regeneration. We were regenerated (reborn spiritually) because God is rich in mercy and because He loved us. Verse six tells us that; *"He raised us up with Christ and seated us with him in the heavenly realms in Christ Jesus,"* and verses seven and ten add: *"[7]in order that in the coming ages he might show the incomparable riches of his grace, expressed in his kindness to us in Christ Jesus"---"[10]For we are God's workmanship,*

*created in Christ Jesus to do good works, which
God prepared in advance for us to do."*

Nowhere in the entire passage does it say that
our salvation, our regeneration, was the result
of God's mercy <u>and</u> our works. On the
contrary, we are saved because of His riches
in mercy <u>and</u> because we are His
workmanship. That in the ages to come
(throughout eternity), His love and mercy will
be on display in our salvation, <u>not</u> His love
and mercy <u>and</u> our good works. According to
verse ten, we will do good works and they
will be on display in the ages to come, but our
good works are a result of His workmanship.
Paul said emphatically: *"⁸For it is by grace
you have been saved, through faith—and this
not from yourselves, it is the gift of God—⁹not
by works, so that no one can boast."* We are
saved by grace (the unmerited favor of God)
and grace alone, not because of any kind of
works. Mankind will not and does not have an
opportunity to boast of his or her salvation.
We are saved by grace, through faith, but even
our faith, according to verse eight, cannot be
claimed as our own work. Faith is the gift of
God.

Isaiah 64:6, speaking of the Israelites (and
prophetically, us*), wrote: "All of us have
become like one who is unclean, and all our*

righteous acts are like filthy rags;" Paul writing of both Jews and Gentile wrote: *"There is no one righteous, not even one"* Romans 3:10. This means that there is none who qualify as being righteous before salvation. To emphasize this further, he added; *"for all have sinned and fall short of the glory of God" Romans 3:23.* No one, no matter how much he (or she) does in their natural state (1 Corinthians 2:14), will ever glorify God by works because everyone before salvation is unfit for His kingdom.

One should be very careful of the traditions of man, or, of additions or deletions of the Scriptures. All writings or traditions, of man should be measured by the Bible, not the Bible by these writings or traditions. According to John 3:1-8, our salvation is because of the work of the Holy Spirit, not because of any works we may have done or will do.

"¹Now there was a man of the Pharisees named Nicodemus, a member of the Jewish ruling council. ²He came to Jesus at night and said, 'Rabbi, we know you are a teacher who has come from God. For no one could perform the miraculous signs you are doing if God were not with him.' ³In reply Jesus declared, 'I tell you the truth, no one can see the kingdom of God unless he is born again.' ⁴'How can a man be

born when he is old?' Nicodemus asked. 'Surely he cannot enter a second time into his mother's womb to be born!' [5]Jesus answered, I tell you the truth, no one can enter the kingdom of God unless he is born of water and the Spirit. [6]Flesh gives birth to flesh, but the Spirit gives birth to spirit. [7]You should not be surprised at my saying, 'You must be born again.' [8]The wind blows wherever it pleases. You hear its sound, but you cannot tell where it comes from or where it is going. So it is with everyone born of the Spirit.'"

God the Father purposed our salvation, God the Son paid the price of our salvation, and the Holy Spirit brought it about in the lives of those He saves. He will not share His glory with anyone else. Romans 8:28-30 is the classic text of God's grace: *"[28]And we know that in all things God works for the good of those who love him, who have been called according to his purpose. [29]For those God foreknew he also predestined to be conformed to the likeness of his Son, that he might be the firstborn among many brothers. [30]And those he predestined, he also called; those he called, he also justified; those he justified, he also glorified."*

God called, justified, and glorified those who are saved in order to bring about His determination (predestination) of conforming

92

us to the image of His Son. This was and is all of God, man's works are nowhere mentioned.

But someone might ask, "What about those persons who are in remote parts of the earth such as jungle peoples who have had no contact with the civilized world, who have had no exposure to the written or spoken Word of God? Are they lost? How can God hold them responsible for not accepting or trusting in Him of whom they knew nothing about?" The answer is that God doesn't hold them responsible for not accepting unrevealed truth. Men are lost because of sin and they are separated from Holy God. More importantly God has separated Himself from fallen (sinful) man. When man's representative (Adam) disobeyed God in the Garden and took of the forbidden fruit he became something other than he had been created. He was created righteous, in a state of innocence, but when he sinned (disobeyed) he became unrighteous. He chose to follow his own will, not God's. He chose to follow a new governing nature, a nature that was controlled by pride and self-rule. Someone might say, "If I had been in the Garden, I would not have sinned, as did Adam." That is an indefensible argument since no one will ever be in the Garden.

That this nature became the nature of all Adam's offspring is proven that even in the most remote part of the earth, men break the rules (the laws) of their given society. Even in our own societies we find people breaking the speed limit, running red lights, parking in handicap zones, even though they are not handicapped and so on. We must even teach our children to be good. It is because of this nature that men sin and they are separated from Holy God and He is separated from sinful men. But thank God, this is not the end of the story. He has taken the salvation of man upon Himself.

CHAPTER 7

SALVATION: THE WORK OF GOD

Many have said that the salvation of the soul (or the spirit) of man is a two-sided work. By this they mean that God does His part for man's salvation, and man does his. Those who hold to this belief say that God has made available through the sacrifice of His anointed (the Lord Jesus Christ) new spiritual life (salvation) and that He offers it to each person who is born into the world. They also say that God cannot redeem man's soul unless man allows it to happen. By this they are implying that God must have the permission of man for salvation to take place.

There are others who believe that new spiritual life is bestowed by God first, followed by a positive response by man to God. Much has been written about this from both perspectives. I personally believe that it is impossible for a spiritually dead person (the condition of all humanity before spiritual life is granted) to make this positive spiritual decision about the Creator, before he or she is made spiritually alive. Paul, in writing to the church at Ephesus affirms this. Paul held that he and his readers were dead toward God until God, Himself, made them alive.

"⁴But because of his great love for us, God, who is rich in mercy, ⁵made us alive with Christ even when we were dead in transgressions" Ephesians 2:4-5. If this is true, does God bestow new spiritual life to everyone? And why doesn't He? Is God fair by bestowing spiritual live to some and not others?

To begin with, John 3:16-17 informs us that God has given a universal call to all, excluding none: *"¹⁶For God so loved the world that he gave his one and only Son, that whoever believes in him shall not perish but have eternal life. ¹⁷For God did not send his Son into the world to condemn the world, but to save the world through him."*

Paul answering the Philippian jailor's question, "What must I do to be saved?" said: "Believe on the Lord Jesus Christ and you will be saved" (Acts 16:30-31). In short, God has offered salvation to all, but even though it has been offered, the forgiveness of sins and salvation does not preclude that the offer has been or will be accepted. God does not force one to accept His offer. Neither does man accept the offer automatically because of his natural state and love of sin. Jesus explained to the visitor Nicodemus:

"¹⁷For God did not send his Son into the world to condemn the world, but to save the world through him. ¹⁸Whoever believes in him is not condemned, but whoever does not believe stands condemned already because he has not believed in the name of God's one and only Son. ¹⁹This is the verdict: Light has come into the world, but men loved darkness instead of light because their deeds were evil. ²⁰Everyone who does evil hates the light, and will not come into the light for fear that his deeds will be exposed" John 3:17-20:

God is just in that He offers salvation to all. To those who come to Him, there is forgiveness and salvation. For those who do not come to Him, His wrath remains on them. In either case, God is righteous. He does not force man to choose either way. The burden, therefore, is on man, not God. However, as Jesus explained in verses 19-20 above, because of his sinful nature, man does not want to give up the appetites and so-called "pleasures of the flesh". The "everyone" of verse 20 includes everyone prior to regeneration. Romans 3:10-12 concludes this as well: *"¹⁰There is no one righteous, not even one; ¹¹there is no one who understands, no one who seeks God. ¹² All have turned away, they have together become worthless; there is no one who does good, not even one."*

Because God is God—just and righteous—one has to be the same in order to be in His presence. That's just a fact. It will not and cannot change. The righteousness of God refers to His absolute holiness. He is just according to His own standards and sinful man—unrighteous and unholy—cannot be in His presence.

As a creation of God, man is responsible to love, obey, and serve God. As a sinner (unregenerate man—natural man), he is responsible to repent and believe the Gospel. However, one must recognize that natural man is unable to love and serve God because as a sinner, he cannot repent and believe. Jesus said in John 6.44, *"No man can come to Me, except the Father which has sent Me draw him."* The heart of the natural man (the man who has not been reborn) is so "desperately wicked" that if left to himself, he would never come to Christ. And again Jesus said in John 5:40, *"You will not come to Me that you might have life."* To become acceptable to God and receive salvation through Christ, he must realize that he is a sinner and that without Christ he is eternally lost. This, however, is impossible since he is born dead towards God (Ephesians 2:1 and 5).

First Corinthians 2:14 states: *"The man without the Spirit does not accept the things that come from the Spirit of God, for they are foolishness to him, and he cannot understand them, because they are spiritually discerned."* A grim picture is painted here. However, God is also a merciful God. He gave up His son for those who are to be redeemed. Jesus Christ (God the Son) gave Himself as the only sacrifice acceptable of God. His sacrifice paid the debt of the sin for those who have or will come to Him.

Charles H. Spurgeon, in his sermon "The Grace Of God" referencing Ephesians 2:8 "By Grace Are You Saved Through Faith," said:

> "I think it well to turn a little to one side that I may ask my listener to observe adoringly the fountain-head of our salvation, which is the grace of God. 'By grace are you saved.' Because God is gracious, sinful men are forgiven, converted, purified, and saved. It is not because of anything in them, or that ever can be in them, that they are saved; but because of the boundless love, goodness, pity, compassion, mercy, and grace of God. Tarry a moment, then, at the wellhead. Behold the pure river of water of life,

as it proceeds out of the throne of God and of the Lamb! What an abyss is the grace of God! Who can measure its breadth? Who can fathom its depth? Like all the rest of the divine attributes, it is infinite. God is full of love, for 'God is love.' God is full of goodness; the very name 'God' is short for 'good.' Unbounded goodness and love enter into the very essence of the Godhead. It is because 'His mercy endures for ever' that men are not destroyed, because 'His compassions fail not' that sinners are brought to Him and forgiven. Remember this; or you may fall into error by fixing your minds so much upon the faith, which is the channel of salvation, as to forget the grace, which is the fountain and source even of faith itself. Faith is the work of God's grace in us. No man can say that Jesus is the Christ but by the Holy Ghost. 'No man comes unto me,' said Jesus 'except the Father which has sent me draw him.' So that faith, which is coming to Christ, is the result of divine drawing."

Without the intervention of God, man is in a terrible predicament—lost and separated from the holiness of God. We read from Revelation 20:11-15: *"[11] Then I saw a great white throne*

100

and him who was seated on it. Earth and sky fled from his presence, and there was no place for them. [12]And I saw the dead, great and small, standing before the throne, and books were opened. Another book was opened, which is the book of life. The dead were judged according to what they had done as recorded in the books. [13]The sea gave up the dead that were in it, and death and Hades gave up the dead that were in them, and each person was judged according to what he had done. [14]Then death and Hades were thrown in to the lake of fire. The lake of fire is the second death. [15]If anyone's name was not found written in the book of life, he was thrown into the lake of fire."

Romans 8:28-30 explains that God is calling man out of spiritual darkness unto Himself, creating in them new spiritual life. *"[28]And we know that in all things God works for the good of those who love him, who have been called according to his purpose. [29]For those God foreknew he also predestined to be conformed to the likeness of his Son, that he might be the firstborn among many brothers. [30]And those he predestined, he also called; those he called, he also justified; those he justified, he also glorified."* Note that this entire passage is in the past tense. God first "efficaciously called" all those He had predestined to be conformed to image of His son. He justified and glorified each one. No activity of man is mentioned.

The question arises, "how did God, in that efficacious call, make unwilling man, in love with his sin, willing to turn from that sin? And how did He make it possible for unrighteous man to be righteous?" An answer to this begins to unfold for us in John 3:1-8:

"¹Now there was a man of the Pharisees named Nicodemus, a member of the Jewish ruling council. ²He came to Jesus at night and said, 'Rabbi, we know you are a teacher who has come from God. For no one could perform the miraculous signs you are doing if God were not with him.' ³In reply Jesus declared, 'I tell you the truth, no one can see the kingdom of God unless he is born again.' ⁴'How can a man be born when he is old?' Nicodemus asked. 'Surely he cannot enter a second time into his mother's womb to be born!' ⁵Jesus answered, 'I tell you the truth, no one can enter the kingdom of God unless he is born of water and the Spirit. ⁶Flesh gives birth to flesh, but the Spirit gives birth to spirit. ⁷You should not be surprised at my saying, You must be born again. ⁸The wind blows wherever it pleases. You hear its sound, but you cannot tell where it comes from or where it is going. So it is with everyone born of the Spirit.'"

God the Holy Spirit overcomes the spiritual darkness of the one who is called and renews his spirit to life. This overcoming of the Holy Spirit follows this process: 1) Man is regenerated (made spiritually alive); 2) he recognizes that he is a sinner; 3) He becomes repentant of his sin; 4) He recognizes that his salvation depends on God's provision, the Lord Jesus Christ, and that he is completely at the mercy of God; 5) He desires to once again have fellowship with God, worshipping Him for who He is; 6) He is washed clean of his sin; and 7) He is sealed and placed by the Holy Spirit into the family of God. John 3:3 tells us that the first thing to happen in this succession is that man is "born again" made spiritually alive: *"I tell you the truth, no one can see the kingdom of God unless he is born again."*

Earlier the question was asked, "How does God make it possible for unrighteous man to be righteous?" Jesus explains in John 3:6: *"Flesh gives birth to flesh, but the Spirit gives birth to spirit."* God the Holy Spirit gives birth to the spirit of man, regenerates one to new spiritual life if you will, making one spiritually alive again. John 3:5 tells us that: *"no one can enter the kingdom of God unless he is born of water and the Spirit"* and Titus 3:5 explains the meaning of this: *"[5] He saved us, not because of righteous things we had done, but because of his mercy. He saved us through the washing of rebirth and renewal by the Holy Spirit."*

The phrase "born of the spirit" in both John 3:3 and 3:5 means to be "born from above. A birth caused and effected from heaven. This was true of a Jewish proselyte named Lydia who worshipped the God of the Hebrews in spiritual darkness yet did not really have spiritual life: *"13On the Sabbath we went outside the city gate to the river, where we expected to find a place of prayer. We sat down and began to speak to the women who had gathered there. 14One of those listening was a woman named Lydia, a dealer in purple cloth from the city of Thyatira, who was a worshiper of God. The Lord opened her heart to respond to Paul's message. 15When she and the members of her household were baptized, she invited us to her home. 'If you consider me a believer in the Lord,' she said, 'come and stay at my house.' And she persuaded us"* Acts 16:13-15.

We see God's triune work in the life of Lydia, and it is the same work exercised in all who come to faith. God the Father has purposed the salvation of those who are redeemed. God the Son has purchased the life of those who are redeemed, and God the Holy Spirit has regenerated/re-birthed those who are redeemed. Nowhere in Scripture do we find God asking man's permission to save him: Ephesians 2:1-9 gives great insight to this:

"¹As for you, you were dead in your transgressions and sins, ²in which you used to live when you followed the ways of this world and of the ruler of the kingdom of the air, the spirit who is now at work in those who are disobedient. ³All of us also lived among them at one time, gratifying the cravings of our sinful nature and following its desires and thoughts. Like the rest, we were by nature objects of wrath. ⁴But because of his great love for us, God, who is rich in mercy, ⁵made us alive with Christ even when we were dead in transgressions—it is by grace you have been saved. ⁶And God raised us up with Christ and seated us with him in the heavenly realms in Christ Jesus, ⁷in order that in the coming ages he might show the incomparable riches of his grace, expressed in his kindness to us in Christ Jesus. ⁸For it is by grace you have been saved, through faith—and this not from yourselves, it is the gift of God—⁹not by works, so that no one can boast. ¹⁰For we are God's workmanship, created in Christ Jesus to do good works, which God prepared in advance for us to do." This passage emphatically states that we were dead toward God (vs.1). We lived to gratify the craving of our sinful natures (vs.3). God chose us in spite of ourselves (vs.4). He gave us the faith necessary to believe (vs.8). It was all of Him, so that we could not boast and say, "I permitted God" (vs.9), and He did this for His glory (vs.7).

Jeremiah 31:31-34 sums up what God is doing for each individual he calls to Himself, as well as what He will do for Israel nationally some day in the future. God will call Israel back to Himself; He will grant them newness of life; He will be their God; He will put His law in their hearts and minds and they will be His people.

"³¹The time is coming, declares the LORD, 'when I will make a new covenant with the house of Israel and with the house of Judah. ³²It will not be like the covenant I made with their forefathers when I took them by the hand to lead them out of Egypt, because they broke my covenant, though I was a husband to them,' declares the LORD. ³³'This is the covenant I will make with the house of Israel after that time,' declares the LORD. 'I will put my law in their minds and write it on their hearts. I will be their God, and they will be my people. ³⁴No longer will a man teach his neighbor, or a man his brother, saying, Know the LORD, because they will all know me, from the least of them to the greatest,' declares the LORD. 'For I will forgive their wickedness and will remember their sins no more.'"

Thank you, Lord, for doing for us as you will do for national Israel, that which we could not have done for ourselves, even if we had wanted to. Thank you for changing our hearts of stone to hearts of flesh, and thank you for granting us newness of life so that we are able to enjoy fellowship with you again.

CHAPTER 8

NO OTHER NAME UNDER HAEAVEN

Man has been led to believe that if a person faithfully believes and commits to a religion, he/she will be accepted by God and granted salvation. While this sounds logical, it is not what the Bible teaches, nor is it what the God of the Bible claims. Jesus said in John 14:6: *"I am the way and the truth and the life. No one comes to the Father except through me."*

The apostle Peter said in Acts 4:12: *"Salvation is found in no one else, for there is no other name under heaven given to men by which we must be saved."*

The apostle Paul wrote in Romans 5: 12-19: *"[12]Therefore, just as sin entered the world through one man, and death through sin, and in this way death came to all men, because all sinned—[13]for before the law was given, sin was in the world. But sin is not taken into account when there is no law. [14]Nevertheless, death reigned from the time of Adam to the time of Moses, even over those who did not sin by breaking a command, as did Adam, who was a pattern of the one to come. [15]But the gift is not like the trespass. For if the many died by the trespass of the one man, how much more did*

God's grace and the gift that came by the grace of the one man, Jesus Christ, overflow to the many! [16]Again, the gift of God is not like the result of the one man's sin: The judgment followed one sin and brought condemnation, but the gift followed many trespasses and brought justification. [17]For if, by the trespass of the one man, death reigned through that one man, how much more will those who receive God's abundant provision of grace and of the gift of righteousness reign in life through the one man, Jesus Christ. [18]Consequently, just as the result of one trespass was condemnation for all men, so also the result of one act of righteousness was justification that brings life for all men. [19]For just as through the disobedience of the one man the many were made sinners, so also through the obedience of the one man the many will be made righteous."

There is a major difference between the majority of religions and biblical Christianity. Religions are works of man and promote the thought that salvation is earned. Christianity, on the other hand, extends God's grace to fallen man. Religion often denies the saving grace of God, and although acknowledges that God extended grace, claims this is in response to the effort of man doing his or her best. Paul wrote:

"¹As for you, you were dead in your transgressions and sins, ²in which you used to live when you followed the ways of this world and of the ruler of the kingdom of the air, the spirit who is now at work in those who are disobedient. ³All of us also lived among them at one time, gratifying the cravings of our sinful nature and following its desires and thoughts. Like the rest, we were by nature objects of wrath. ⁴But because of his great love for us, God, who is rich in mercy, ⁵made us alive with Christ even when we were dead in transgressions—it is by grace you have been saved" Ephesians 2:1-5.

Paul went on to write: *"⁸It is by grace you have been saved, through faith—and this not from yourselves, it is the gift of God—⁹not by works, so that no one can boast"* He gave the reason of God's grace in verse 7: *"in order that in the coming ages he might show the incomparable riches of his grace, expressed in his kindness to us in Christ Jesus,"* and added in verse 10: *"For we are God's workmanship, created in Christ Jesus to do good works, which God prepared in advance for us to do."*

A religion based on works attempts to rob God of the glory justly due Him. This will not prevail throughout the ages to come. Instead, His glory will be recognized by His kindness to the redeemed, accomplished by the faithfulness of the Lord Jesus Christ. Christ's sacrifice removed God's wrath from those brought to salvation. For those who are not redeemed, God's wrath remains. Revelation 20:11-15: tells of the consequence of that wrath: *"[11]Then I saw a great white throne and him who was seated on it. Earth and sky fled from his presence, and there was no place for them. [12]And I saw the dead, great and small, standing before the throne, and books were opened. Another book was opened, which is the book of life. The dead were judged according to what they had done as recorded in the books. [13]The sea gave up the dead that were in it, and death and Hades gave up the dead that were in them, and each person was judged according to what he had done. [14]Then death and Hades were thrown into the lake of fire. The lake of fire is the second death. [15]If anyone's name was not found written in the book of life, he was thrown into the lake of fire."*

Paul said of his fellow Jews: *"[1]Brothers, my heart's desire and prayer to God for the Israelites is that they may be saved. [2]For I can testify about them that they are zealous for God, but their zeal is not based on knowledge. [3]Since they did not know the righteousness that comes from God and sought to establish their own, they did not submit to God's righteousness. [4]Christ is the end of the law so that there may*

be righteousness for everyone who believes"
Romans 10: 1-4.

Jesus' testimony to us through Nicodemus is:

"³No one can see the kingdom of God unless he is born again, ⁵nor can one enter the kingdom of God unless he is born of water and the Spirit" John 3:3 and 5.

Returning to Paul's letter to the Romans, we read that salvation cannot be gained by keeping the law but through Jesus Christ, the God/man. *"⁵Moses describes in this way the righteousness that is by the law: 'The man who does these things will live by them.'⁶But the righteousness that is by faith says: 'Do not say in your heart, Who will ascend into heaven?' (that is, to bring Christ down) ⁷or 'Who will descend into the deep?'(that is, to bring Christ up from the dead). ⁸But what does it say? 'The word is near you; it is in your mouth and in your heart,' that is, the word of faith we are proclaiming: ⁹That if you confess with your mouth, 'Jesus is Lord,' and believe in your heart that God raised him from the dead, you will be saved. ¹⁰For it is with your heart that you believe and are justified, and it is with your mouth that you confess and are saved. ¹¹As the Scripture says, 'Anyone who trusts in him will never be put to shame.' ¹²For there is no difference between Jew and Gentile—the same Lord is Lord of all and richly blesses all who* *call on him, ¹³for, 'Everyone who calls on the name of the Lord will be saved.'" Romans* 10:5-13.

Paul was called by God to proclaim His Word so that in hearing it, people would be saved. Although he ministered to the Gentiles, Paul always carried in his heart a love for his own people, the Jews. The Jews could not be saved by their religion, nor could any religion of the Gentiles save them. Only the Lord Jesus Christ could accomplish this. Paul, after many years of faithful service to the Lord, was martyred because of his faithfulness. In fact, his own people, the Jews, had him killed because they rejected the truth and dogmatically held to their religion. It is very dangerous to believe that religion can save. According to the Bible, salvation is only accomplished by the work of Jesus Christ.

The writer of Hebrews puts it this way:

"¹The law is only a shadow of the good things that are coming—not the realities themselves. For this reason it can never, by the same sacrifices repeated endlessly year after year, make perfect those who draw near to worship. ²If it could, would they not have stopped being offered? For the worshipers would have been cleansed once for all, and would no longer have

114

felt guilty for their sins. ³But those sacrifices are an annual reminder of sins, ⁴because it is impossible for the blood of bulls and goats to take away sins. ⁵Therefore, when Christ came into the world, he said: 'Sacrifice and offering you did not desire, but a body you prepared for me; ⁶ with burnt offerings and sin offerings you were not pleased. ⁷Then I said, Here I am—it is written about me in the scroll—I have come to do your will, O God.' ⁸First he said, 'Sacrifices and offerings, burnt offerings and sin offerings you did not desire, nor were you pleased with them' (although the law required them to be made). ⁹Then he said, 'Here I am, I have come to do your will.' He sets aside the first to establish the second. ¹⁰And by that will, we have been made holy through the sacrifice of the body of Jesus Christ once for all. ¹¹Day after day every priest stands and performs his religious duties; again and again he offers the same sacrifices which can never take away sins. ¹²But when this priest had offered for all time one sacrifice for sins, he sat down at the right hand of God" Hebrews 10:1-12.

Many people deny this truth and seek to satisfy Holy God by religious works, but as Paul and Silas testified to the Philippian jailor: "Believe in the Lord Jesus Christ and you will be saved-you and your household" *Acts 16:31.*

Have you trusted in the Lord Jesus Christ, dear reader, for your salvation? John 3:18 and 3:36 unequivocally state:

3:18 *"Whoever believes in Him is not condemned, but whoever does not believe stands condemned already because he has not believed in the name of God's one and only Son."*

3:36 *"Whoever believes in the Son has eternal life, but whosoever rejects the Son will not see life, for God's wrath remains on Him.'*

God is assuredly a God of Love. This was demonstrated by what God the Father gave for man's salvation (His only begotten Son). God the Son demonstrated God's love when He freely gave of Himself to suffer and die on the cross to satisfy the righteousness of God. God the Holy Spirit continues to demonstrate God's love as He ceaselessly roams the earth regenerating and sealing those God the Father calls to salvation.

CHAPTER 9

BORN AGAIN

Many today claim to have had a "born again" experience. When asked what the term means, there are a wide range of answers given. The Bible, however, has one definition of being "born again": to be born from above. John 3:1-8 states: *"¹Now there was a man of the Pharisees named Nicodemus, a member of the Jewish ruling council. ²He came to Jesus at night and said, 'Rabbi, we know you are a teacher who has come from God. For no one could perform the miraculous signs you are doing if God were not with him.' ³In reply Jesus declared, 'I tell you the truth, no one can see the kingdom of God unless he is born again.' ⁴'How can a man be born when he is old?' Nicodemus asked. 'Surely he cannot enter a second time into his mother's womb to be born!' ⁵Jesus answered, 'I tell you the truth, no one can enter the kingdom of God unless he is born of water and the Spirit. ⁶Flesh gives birth to flesh, but the Spirit gives birth to spirit. ⁷You should not be surprised at my saying, You must be born again. ⁸The wind blows wherever it pleases. You hear its sound, but you cannot tell where it comes from or where it is going. So it is with everyone born of the Spirit.'"*

Jesus told Nicodemus (and us) that for a person to understand (see) or enter the kingdom of God, he or she must be born again. This is not a term to be taken lightly, but deeply considered. Some may say there are many ways to heaven, but Jesus said one must be "born again" to enter. He further explains in verse 6: *"Flesh gives birth to flesh, but the Spirit gives birth to spirit."*

A definition of terms found in verse 6 may prove helpful at this point. "Flesh" is defined as: the corporal part of man, the body of man, the natural man. "Spirit" refers to the Holy Spirit when a capital letter is used. The second use of the word "spirit" (lower case) is the spirit of man. Based on these definitions, verse 6 means that the Holy Spirit of God gives birth (in the sense of regeneration) to the spirit of man. Being born again is not a new physical rebirth, but a rebirth of the inward man, a rebirth of one's spirit. The logical question then becomes: How does the Holy Spirit birth the spirit of man? To answer this question, we should first consider man. Three passages shed light on the answer:

Genesis 2:7 *"The LORD God formed the man from the dust of the ground and breathed into his nostrils the breath of life, and the man became a living being."*

Hebrews 4:*12 "For the word of God is living and active. Sharper than any double-edged sword, it penetrates even to dividing soul and spirit, joints and marrow; it judges the thoughts and attitudes of the heart."*

Genesis 2:16-17 *"¹⁶And the LORD God commanded the man, 'You are free to eat from any tree in the garden; ¹⁷but you must not eat from the tree of the knowledge of good and evil, for when you eat of it you will surely die.'"*

From these passages, we learn that man was born with a body, soul, and spirit. We also discover that God imposed a condition, a prohibition, and a judgment. The condition was that man should obey God's authority. The prohibition stated that man was not to disobey God or partake of the tree of the knowledge of good and evil. The judgment involved death if they disobeyed. According to verse 17, the sentence was an immediate spiritual death and an eventual physical death. The spirit of man gave him God-consciousness – a desire to know and fellowship with God and the ability to communicate. But when Adam disobeyed, he became dead toward God. Just as physical death separates one from all that is living, disobedience and sin separated Adam and all mankind from God. A God consciousness, a desire for fellowship, and communication all needed to be restored. This restitution only comes from being "born again," a rebirth of our spirits toward God. Still, the question remains: How does the Holy Spirit birth the spirit of man? Jesus gives a veiled answer to this question in John 3:7- 8: *"7You should not be surprised at my saying, You must be born again. 8The wind blows wherever it pleases. You hear its sound, but you cannot tell where it comes from or where it is going. So it is with everyone born of the Spirit."*

The wind begins and ends unhampered. In the same way, the Holy Spirit moves among men as He pleases, when He pleases, and where He pleases. This is not without purpose, however. He regenerates to newness of spiritual life those to whom He has been sent. Romans 8:28-30 tells us that God calls one to salvation for the purpose of conforming him or her into the image of the Lord Jesus Christ. *"28And we know that in all things God works for the good of those who love him, who have been called according to his purpose. 29For those God foreknew he also predestined to be conformed to the likeness of his Son, that he might be the firstborn among many brothers. 30And those he predestined, he also called; those he called, he also justified; those he justified, he also glorified."*

Being "born again" begins with the efficacious calling of God so that those called will be of many brothers (verse 29), spiritual brothers of the Lord Jesus Himself. One might ask, "What does it mean to be "called"? When one is called, he or she is called *from* something *to* something different. In the case of the redeemed, one is called from spiritual darkness to new spiritual life. One might ask, "How does God call one out of spiritual darkness?" It is by the overwhelming convincing and convicting of the Holy Spirit who accomplishes this by illuminating the truth about Jesus Christ to the darkened heart. The truth about Jesus delivered by the power and the authority of the Holy Spirit brings conviction and subsequently, commitment. Hebrews 4:12 says of the Word: *"For the word of God is living and active. Sharper than any double-edged sword, it penetrates even to dividing soul and spirit, joints and marrow; it judges the thoughts and attitudes of the heart,"* 1 Peter 1.23 tells us that, *"we have been born again, not of perishable seed, but of imperishable, through the living and enduring word of God."*

Being "born again" begins with the call of God. The Holy Spirit then illuminates the truth about Jesus to the heart of the one who is to be born again. John 16:8-11 tells us this illumination is not passive, but has a determination. *"⁸He (the Holy Spirit) will convict the world of guilt in regard to sin and righteousness and judgment: ⁹in regard to sin, because men do not believe in me; ¹⁰in regard to righteousness, because I am going to the Father, where you can see me no longer; ¹¹and in regard to judgment, because the prince of this world now stands condemned."*

It is by the determined will of God that one is born again, mitigated by His love and grace. Consider Ephesians 2:8: *"For by grace are ye saved through faith; and that not of yourselves: it is the gift of God."* This passage tells us that we are saved by the grace of God and that He gives us the faith necessary to believe Him and what is written about Him. Hebrews 4:12 tells us that His Word, the Scriptures, *"are more powerful than any two-edged sword"* able to convict and convince us of our sin and our need to be delivered." 1 Peter 1:23 states: we are *"born again by the word of God."* And Titus 3:5 emphasizes that it is *"Not by works of righteousness which we have done, but according to his mercy he saved us, by the washing of regeneration, and renewing of the Holy Ghost."*

Notice when this takes place!

"¹As for you, you were dead in your transgressions and sins, ²in which you used to live when you followed the ways of this world and of the ruler of the kingdom of the air, the spirit who is now at work in those who are disobedient. ³All of us also lived among them at one time, gratifying the cravings of our sinful nature and following its desires and thoughts. Like the rest, we were by nature objects of wrath. ⁴But because of his great love for us, God, who is rich in mercy, ⁵made us alive with Christ even when we were dead in transgressions—it is by grace you have been saved" Ephesians 2:1-5.

Being "born again" begins with the work of the Holy Spirit while we are in a dead (separated) state toward God.

In summary then, being "born again" is the renewal of spiritual life. Not a re-creation of man's spirit because it exists from time of birth, but a renewal of a recognition of True God, a desire to please Him and a desire to serve Him. Also, an awareness of sin is reawakened and a desire to flee from it, bringing confession and repentance. If these things are the makeup of one's life, he or she has been born again. Spiritual rebirth is by the will of God, not the will of man. John 1:11-13 states:

"[11]He came to that which was his own, but his own did not receive him. [12]Yet to all who received him, to those who believed in his name, he gave the right to become children of God— [13]children born not of natural descent, nor of human decision or a husband's will, but born of God."

Being born again brings change to one's life. Consider Ephesians 5:1-10: *"[1]Be imitators of God, therefore, as dearly loved children [2]and live a life of love, just as Christ loved us and gave himself up for us as a fragrant offering and sacrifice to God. [3]But among you there must not be even a hint of sexual immorality, or of any kind of impurity, or of greed, because these are improper for God's holy people. [4]Nor should there be obscenity, foolish talk or coarse joking, which are out of place, but rather thanksgiving. [5]For of this you can be sure: No immoral, impure or greedy person—such a man is an idolater—has any inheritance in the kingdom of Christ and of God. [6]Let no one deceive you with empty words, for because of such things God's wrath comes on those who are disobedient. [7]Therefore do not be partners with them. [8]For you were once darkness, but now you are light in the Lord. Live as children of light [9](for the fruit of the light consists in all goodness, righteousness and truth) [10]and find out what pleases the Lord."*

Some may assert that if one recites a certain prayer, walks down an aisle, or is baptized by water, he or she is born again. While this may be true of those who have been born again, these things alone do not preclude that one has truly been born again. A changed life is the evidence of true rebirth.

Ephesians 2:10: *"For we are God's workman-ship, created in Christ Jesus to do good works, which God prepared in advance for us to do."*

Galatians 5:19-24: *"[19]The acts of the sinful nature are obvious: sexual immorality, impurity and debauchery; [20] idolatry and witchcraft; hatred, discord, jealousy, fits of rage, selfish ambition, dissensions, factions [21]and envy; drunkenness, orgies, and the like. I warn you, as I did before, that those who live like this will not inherit the kingdom of God. [22]But the fruit of the Spirit is love, joy, peace, patience, kindness, goodness, faithfulness, [23]gentleness and self-control. Against such things there is no law. [24]Those who belong to Christ Jesus have crucified the sinful nature with its passions and desires."*

If a person is truly born again, there will be a change in his or her life. Without a changed life, there has been no rebirth. The apostle John wrote of several changes that God brings about in the life of one who is born again. We read from his first letter:

2:3-6: Obey His commandments. *"³Now by this we may be sure that we know him, if we obey his commandments. ⁴Whoever says, 'I have come to know him,' but does not obey his commandments, is a liar, and in such a person the truth does not exist; ⁵but whoever obeys his word, truly in this person the love of God has reached perfection. By this we may be sure that we are in him: ⁶whoever says, 'I abide in him,' ought to walk just as he walked."*

2:8-11: Loving one's brother. *"⁸Yet I am writing you a new commandment that is true in him and in you, because the darkness is passing away and the true light is already shining. ⁹Whoever says, 'I am in the light,' while hating a brother or sister, is still in the darkness. ¹⁰Whoever loves a brother or sister lives in the light, and in such a person there is no cause for stumbling. ¹¹But whoever hates another believer is in the darkness, walks in the darkness, and does not know the way to go, because the darkness has brought on blindness."*

3:14-21: *"¹⁴We know that we have passed from death to life because we love one another. Whoever does not love abides in death. ¹⁵All who hate a brother or sister are murderers, and you know that murderers do not have eternal* *life abiding in them. ¹⁶We know love by this, that he laid down his life for us—and we ought to lay down our lives for one another. ¹⁷How does God's love abide in anyone who has the world's goods and sees a brother or sister in need and yet refuses help? ¹⁸Little children, let us love, not in word or speech, but in truth and action. ¹⁹And by this we will know that we are from the truth and will reassure our hearts before him ²⁰whenever our hearts condemn us; for God is greater than our hearts, and he knows everything. ²¹Beloved, if our hearts do not condemn us, we have boldness before God."*

2:15-17: Love not the world. *"¹⁵Do not love the world or the things in the world. The love of the Father is not in those who love the world; ¹⁶for all that is in the world—the desire of the flesh, the desire of the eyes, the pride in riches—comes not from the Father but from the world. ¹⁷And the world and its desire are passing away, but those who do the will of God live forever."*

2:21-25: Acknowledge Jesus as God in the flesh. *"²¹I write to you, not because you do not know the truth, but because you know it, and you know that no lie comes from the truth. ²²Who is the liar but the one who denies that Jesus is the Christ? This is the antichrist, the one who denies the Father and the Son. ²³No one who denies the Son has the Father;*

everyone who confesses the Son has the Father also. *²⁴Let what you heard from the beginning abide in you. If what you heard from the beginning abides in you, then you will abide in the Son and in the Father. ²⁵And this is what he has promised us, eternal life."*

5:1-5: *"¹Everyone who believes that Jesus is the Christ has been born of God, and everyone who loves the parent loves the child. ²By this we know that we love the children of God, when we love God and obey his commandments. ³For the love of God is this, that we obey his commandments. And his commandments are not burdensome, ⁴for whatever is born of God conquers the world. And this is the victory that conquers the world, our faith. ⁵Who is it that conquers the world but the one who believes that Jesus is the Son of God?"*

3:9-10: Does not continue in sin. *"⁹Those who have been born of God do not sin, because God's seed abides in them; they cannot sin, because they have been born of God. ¹⁰The children of God and the children of the devil are revealed in this way: all who do not do what is right are not from God, nor are those who do not love their brothers and sisters."*

Because of these assurances John wrote: *"I write these things to you who believe in the*

name of the Son of God, so that you may know
that you have eternal life" 1 John 5:13.

If God has truly worked these things in one's life, he or she is born again. One should ask himself or herself, "Have I been 'born again' according to John's Spirit-inspired critique? If one is not sure, one should cry out to God for forgiveness and mercy, He will answer with love and grace. Jesus said: *"I am the bread of life. Whoever comes to me will never be hungry, and whoever believes in me will never be thirsty. 36But I said to you that you have seen me and yet do not believe. 37Everything that the Father gives me will come to me, and anyone who comes to me I will never drive away; 38for I have come down from heaven, not to do my own will, but the will of him who sent me. 39And this is the will of him who sent me, that I should lose nothing of all that he has given me, but raise it up on the last day"* John 6:35-39. It is impossible for Jesus to lose one that has been given to Him by the Father. Further He says He will never drive one away that has come to Him. The question is, "Have you truly come to Him for salvation?" If you have, your life will be consistent with those criteria given by John the apostle.

May God bless you as you consider these things.

CHAPTER 10

THE EMPTY CROSS

The cross of Jesus Christ is displayed in various ways. This is a reminder that He suffered and died for mankind. Many times we see it occupied by a replica of Christ's body. In other displays, the cross is vacant. This conveys God's acceptance of His Son's sacrifice as payment for man's sin. Its emptiness testifies to the belief that His death was the beginning of man's atonement. For the apostle Paul, the empty cross and the empty tomb present the risen Christ. In his letter to the Romans, he states: *"He was delivered over to death for our sins and was raised to life for our justification" Romans 14:25.*

Paul further affirms the absolute necessity of Christ's resurrection in 1 Corinthians 15.12-23: [12] *"But if it is preached that Christ has been raised from the dead, how can some of you say that there is no resurrection of the dead?* [13] *If there is no resurrection of the dead, then not even Christ has been raised.* [14] *And if Christ has not been raised, our preaching is useless and so is your faith.* [15] *More than that, we are then found to be false witnesses about God, for we have testified about God that he raised Christ from the dead. But he did not raise him if in fact* *the dead are not raised. ^{16}For if the dead are not raised, then Christ has not been raised either. ^{17}And if Christ has not been raised, your faith is futile; you are still in your sins. ^{18}Then those also who have fallen asleep in Christ are lost. ^{19}If only for this life we have hope in Christ, we are to be pitied more than all men. ^{20}But Christ has indeed been raised from the dead, the firstfruits of those who have fallen asleep. ^{21}For since death came through a man, the resurrection of the dead comes also through a man. ^{22}For as in Adam all die, so in Christ all will be made alive. ^{23}But each in his own turn: Christ, the firstfruits; then, when he comes, those who belong to him."*

The information the apostle John was instructed to relay in the book of Revelation gives testimony that Jesus did not remain in the tomb. Revelation 1.9-18: *"^{9} I John, your brother and companion in the suffering and kingdom and patient endurance that are ours in Jesus, was on the island of Patmos because of the word of God and the testimony of Jesus. ^{10} On the Lord's Day I was in the Spirit, and I heard behind me a loud voice like a trumpet, ^{11}which said: 'Write on a scroll what you see and send it to the seven churches: to Ephesus, Smyrna, Pergamum, Thyatira, Sardis, Philadelphia and Laodicea.' ^{12}I turned around to see the voice that was speaking to me. And when I turned I saw seven golden lampstands, ^{13}and among the lampstands was someone 'like* *a son of man,' dressed in a robe reaching down to his feet and with a golden sash around his chest. [14]His head and hair were white like wool, as white as snow, and his eyes were like blazing fire. [15]His feet were like bronze glowing in a furnace, and his voice was like the sound of rushing waters. [16]In his right hand he held seven stars, and out of his mouth came a sharp double-edged sword. His face was like the sun shining in all its brilliance. [17]When I saw him, I fell at his feet as though dead. Then he placed his right hand on me and said: 'Do not be afraid. I am the First and the Last. [18]I am the Living One; I was dead, and behold I am alive for ever and ever! And I hold the keys of death and Hades'"*

In Chapters 4 and 5 John was caused to write:

Chapter 4: *"[1]After this I looked, and there before me was a door standing open in heaven. And the voice I had first heard speaking to me like a trumpet said, 'Come up here, and I will show you what must take place after this.' [2]At once I was in the Spirit, and there before me was a throne in heaven with someone sitting on it. [3]And the one who sat there had the appearance of jasper and carnelian. A rainbow, resembling an emerald, encircled the throne. [4]Surrounding the throne were twenty-four other thrones, and seated on them were twenty-four elders. They were dressed in white and had crowns of gold on their heads. [5]From the throne came flashes of lightning, rumblings and peals of thunder. Before the throne, seven lamps were* blazing. *These are the seven spirits of God. ⁶Also before the throne there was what looked like a sea of glass, clear as crystal. In the center, around the throne, were four living creatures, and they were covered with eyes, in front and in back. ⁷The first living creature was like a lion, the second was like an ox, the third had a face like a man, the fourth was like a flying eagle. ⁸Each of the four living creatures had six wings and was covered with eyes all around, even under his wings. Day and night they never stop saying: 'Holy, holy, holy is the Lord God Almighty, who was, and is, and is to come.' ⁹Whenever the living creatures give glory, honor and thanks to him who sits on the throne and who lives for ever and ever, ¹⁰the twenty-four elders fall down before him who sits on the throne, and worship him who lives for ever and ever. They lay their crowns before the throne and say: ¹¹ You are worthy, our Lord and God, to receive glory and honor and power, for you created all things, and by your will they were created and have their being.'"*

Chapter 5: *"¹Then I saw in the right hand of him who sat on the throne a scroll with writing on both sides and sealed with seven seals. ²And I saw a mighty angel proclaiming in a loud voice, 'Who is worthy to break the seals and open the scroll?' ³But no one in heaven or on earth or under the earth could open the scroll or even look inside it. ⁴I wept and wept because no one was found who was worthy to open the* scroll or look inside. *⁵Then one of the elders said to me, 'Do not weep! See, the Lion of the tribe of Judah, the Root of David, has triumphed. He is able to open the scroll and its seven seals.' ⁶Then I saw a Lamb, looking as if it had been slain, standing in the center of the throne, encircled by the four living creatures and the elders. He had seven horns and seven eyes, which are the seven spirits of God sent out into all the earth. ⁷He came and took the scroll from the right hand of him who sat on the throne. ⁸And when he had taken it, the four living creatures and the twenty-four elders fell down before the Lamb. Each one had a harp and they were holding golden bowls full of incense, which are the prayers of the saints. ⁹And they sang a new song: 'You are worthy to take the scroll and to open its seals, because you were slain, and with your blood you purchased men for God from every tribe and language and people and nation. ¹⁰You have made them to be a kingdom and priests to serve our God, and they will reign on the earth.' ¹¹Then I looked and heard the voice of many angels, numbering thousands upon thousands, and ten thousand times ten thousand. They encircled the throne and the living creatures and the elders. ¹²In a loud voice they sang: 'Worthy is the Lamb, who was slain, to receive power and wealth and wisdom and strength and honor and glory and praise!' ¹³Then I heard every creature in heaven and on earth and under the earth and on the sea, and all that is in*

*them, singing: 'To him who sits on the throne
and to the Lamb be praise and honor and glory
and power, for ever and ever!'* [14]*The four living
creatures said, 'Amen,' and the elders fell down
and worshiped."*

Born-again Christians see not only the empty
cross, they see the empty tomb. This is God's
testimony that He has accepted Christ's
sacrifice for the atonement of the sin of those
He redeems. Hebrews 10:1-12 affirms this
truth: *"*[1]*The law is only a shadow of the good
things that are coming—not the realities
themselves. For this reason it can never, by the
same sacrifices repeated endlessly year after
year, make perfect those who draw near to
worship.* [2]*If it could, would they not have
stopped being offered? For the worshipers
would have been cleansed once for all, and
would no longer have felt guilty for their sins.*
[3]*But those sacrifices are an annual reminder of
sins,* [4]*because it is impossible for the blood of
bulls and goats to take away sins.* [5]*Therefore,
when Christ came into the world, he
said:'Sacrifice and offering you did not desire,
but a body you prepared for me;* [6]*with burnt
offerings and sin offerings you were not
pleased'.* [7]*Then I said, 'Here I am—it is written
about me in the scroll— I have come to do your
will, O God.'*

⁸First he said, 'Sacrifices and offerings, burnt offerings and sin offerings you did not desire, nor were you pleased with them' (although the law required them to be made). ⁹Then he said, 'Here I am, I have come to do your will.' He sets aside the first to establish the second. ¹⁰And by that will, we have been made holy through the sacrifice of the body of Jesus Christ once for all. ¹¹Day after day every priest stands and performs his religious duties; again and again he offers the same sacrifices, which can never take away sins. ¹²But when this priest had offered for all time one sacrifice for sins, he sat down at the right hand of God."

Because of His faithfulness, God the Father has made God the Son Savior and Lord. This could not be true if Jesus had remained in the tomb. Why is all this so important? Because man is lost and eternally separated from God. He must bear the consequence of his sin unless that consequence is transferred to another. This is what God has done. In His mercy, God has transferred the penalty of the sin (spiritual death) of the redeemed to Christ.

The writer of Hebrews was led by the Holy Spirit to give the following warning in Chapter 3: *"¹Therefore, holy brothers, who share in the heavenly calling, fix your thoughts on Jesus, the apostle and high priest whom we confess. ²He was faithful to the one who appointed him, just as Moses was faithful in all God's house. ³Jesus has been found worthy of greater honor than Moses, just as the builder of a house has greater honor than the house itself. ⁴For every house is built by someone, but God is the builder of everything. ⁵Moses was faithful as a servant in all God's house, testifying to what would be said in the future. ⁶But Christ is faithful as a son over God's house. And we are his house, if we hold on to our courage and the hope of which we boast. ⁷So, as the Holy Spirit says: 'Today, if you hear his voice, ⁸do not harden your hearts as you did in the rebellion, during the time of testing in the desert, ⁹ where your fathers tested and tried me and for forty years saw what I did. ¹⁰ That is why I was angry with that generation, and I said, Their hearts are always going astray, and they have not known my ways.¹¹ So I declared on oath in my anger, They shall never enter my rest.' ¹²See to it, brothers, that none of you has a sinful, unbelieving heart that turns away from the living God. ¹³But encourage one another daily, as long as it is called Today, so that none of you may be hardened by sin's deceitfulness. ¹⁴We have come to share in Christ if we hold firmly till the end the confidence we had at first. ¹⁵As has just been said: 'Today, if you hear his voice, do not harden your hearts as you did in the rebellion.' ¹⁶Who were they who heard and rebelled? Were they not all those Moses led out of Egypt? ¹⁷And with whom was he angry for forty years? Was it not with those who sinned,* *whose bodies fell in the desert? ^{18}And to whom did God swear that they would never enter his rest if not to those who disobeyed? ^{19}So we see that they were not able to enter, because of their unbelief."*

In this chapter the writer continues his thoughts from chapters one and two. He begins by challenging his believing Jewish brothers to consider the Apostle and High Priest of their profession, the Lord Jesus Christ, confirming to them His Son-ship. In verse seven, he begins to address his earthly racial brothers (those who have not come to faith in the Lord Jesus) and warns them not to delay in turning to Christ as their forefathers delayed trusting God's leading in the wilderness. Their forefathers were not allowed to enter the rest of God (the promised land). In much the same way, the recipients of the letter of Hebrews would not enter into the rest of redemption if they did not turn to Christ. Not trusting Christ would end in a very sad reality, never being able to enter the rest of heaven. Because the cross and the tomb are both empty no one has to remain separated from God. Jesus made it possible for man to be brought back into fellowship with God, his Creator.

CHAPTER 11

ETERNAL SECURITY

Why are some Christians under the delusion that they could lose their salvation? After all, Jesus said: *"²⁷My sheep listen to my voice; I know them, and they follow me. ²⁸ I give them eternal life, and they shall never perish; no one can snatch them out of my hand. ²⁹My Father, who has given them to me, is greater than all; no one can snatch them out of my Father's hand. ³⁰ I and the Father are one" John 10:27-30.*

In examining this passage we find....

1) God the Father gave God the Son certain ones to be His sheep.

2) Jesus gave to His sheep eternal life.

3) His sheep shall never perish.

4) God is greater than all and no one is able to pluck (remove) a child (sheep) from His hand.

Because the passage emphatically confirms that those who are the Lord's (are His sheep) are kept by the authority (power) of both Jesus (God the Son) and God the Father, not independently, but in co-operation with one another, one needs never fear losing his or her salvation. Perhaps it is such passages as Hebrews 6:1-12 and Matthew 10:22-23 that cause the wavering Christian confusion and consternation. Both passages, when mis-interpreted, could cause one great concern, but when properly understood, all fear should be erased.

Hebrews 6:1-12: *"[1]Therefore let us leave the elementary teachings about Christ and go on to maturity, not laying again the foundation of repentance from acts that lead to death, and of faith in God, [2]instruction about baptisms, the laying on of hands, the resurrection of the dead, and eternal judgment. [3]And God permitting, we will do so. [4]It is impossible for those who have once been enlightened, who have tasted the heavenly gift, who have shared in the Holy Spirit, [5]who have tasted the goodness of the word of God and the powers of the coming age, [6]if they fall away, to be brought back to repentance, because to their loss they are crucifying the Son of God all over again and subjecting him to public disgrace. [7]Land that drinks in the rain often falling on it and that produces a crop useful to those for whom it is farmed receives the blessing of God. [8]But land that produces thorns and thistles is worthless*

142

and is in danger of being cursed. In the end it will be burned. ⁹Even though we speak like this, dear friends, we are confident of better things in your case—things that accompany salvation. ¹⁰God is not unjust; he will not forget your work and the love you have shown him as you have helped his people and continue to help them. ¹¹We want each of you to show this same diligence to the very end, in order to make your hope sure. ¹²We do not want you to become lazy, but to imitate those who through faith and patience inherit what has been promised."

On the surface, it may appear that one could lose his or her salvation. However, there is nothing in these verses that speaks of a born-again person losing his or her salvation. If salvation could be lost, it would be terrible news, for according to the passage one could never approach salvation again. The passage states, "It is impossible (not improbable, but impossible) to renew them again to repentance."

One should keep in mind, the writer of this letter was writing to a diverse group of people, not just Jewish converts to Christianity. He was also addressing Jews who had approached Christianity but after considering the cost had backed away.

John Walvoord (The Bible Knowledge Commentary/Walvoord & Zuck) writes: This passage has been interpreted in four ways:

1) "That the danger of a Christian losing his or her salvation is described, a view rejected because of many biblical assurances that salvation is a work of God which cannot be reversed;

2) That the warning is against mere profession of faith short of salvation, or tasting but not really partaking of salvation;

3) That hypothetically if a Christian could lose his or her salvation, there is no provision for repentance;

4) That a warning is given of the danger of a Christian moving from a position of true faith and life to the extent of becoming disqualified for further service."

In light of passages such as John 10:27-30 (quoted above) and Ephesians chapters 1 and 2, etc. the phrases:

1)   *Who have once been enlightened;*

2) *Who have tasted the heavenly gift;*

3) *Who have shared in the Holy Spirit;*

4) *Who have tasted the goodness of the Word of God and the powers of the coming age; and*

5) *If they shall fall away, to renew them again unto repentance; seeing they crucify to themselves the Son of God afresh, and put him to an open shame;*

are best understood to apply to those who approached Christianity, but backed away when they considered the cost.

The words "fall away" cannot refer to loss of eternal life. This would be in contradiction to John 10:27-30 and Hebrews 6:1-12. These verses emphatically declare the inalienable possession of eternal life for those who trust Christ. The writer of our text in Hebrews evidently has in mind defection from the faith, that is, apostasy or withdrawal from the Christian profession. Remember, profession does not mean possession.

Jesus said about those who professed but did not possess:

"21Not everyone who says to me, 'Lord, Lord,' will enter the kingdom of heaven, but only he who does the will of my Father who is in heaven. 22Many will say to me on that day, 'Lord, Lord, did we not prophesy in your name, and in your name drive out demons and perform many miracles?' 23Then I will tell them plainly, 'I never knew you. Away from me, you evildoers!' 24'Therefore everyone who hears these words of mine and puts them into practice is like a wise man who built his house on the rock. 25The rain came down, the streams rose, and the winds blew and beat against that house; yet it did not fall, because it had its foundation on the rock. 26But everyone who hears these words of mine and does not put them into practice is like a foolish man who built his house on sand. 27The rain came down, the streams rose, and the winds blew and beat against that house, and it fell with a great crash'" Matthew 7:21-27.

The writer clearly makes a distinction between whom he has just been talking about in the previous verses and of those of his attention in verse 9. *"Even though we speak like this, dear friends, we are confident of better things in your case—things that accompany salvation."*

John MacArthur, in his commentary on the book of Hebrews, writes:

> We should notice that this passage makes no reference at all to salvation. There is no mention of justification, sanctification, the new birth, or regeneration. Those who have been enlightened are not spoken of as born again, made holy, or made righteous. None of the normal New Testament terminology for salvation is used.

> The enlightenment spoken of here has to do with intellectual perception of spiritual, biblical truth. In the Septuagint, the Greek word (phôtizô) several times is translated "to give light by knowledge or teaching." It means to be mentally aware of something, to be instructed, informed. It carries no connotation of response—of acceptance or rejection, belief or disbelief.

> Partakers (Greek, metochos) have to do with association, not possession. These Jews had never possessed the Holy Spirit; they simply were around when He was around.

The writer of Hebrews gives a clear warning that should be taken to heart. It is this: "There is no repentance" for anyone if they have rejected the repentance that is given through the Lord Jesus Christ. They were to leave the principles of the doctrine of Christ and go on to maturity, *"not laying again the foundation of repentance from dead works, and of faith toward God, reverting back and relying on the doctrine of baptisms, and of laying on of hands, and of eternal judgment"* Hebrews 6:1-2. The author is exhorting the Hebrews to go on unto Christ to whom all these doctrines pointed. "For it was impossible for those who were once enlightened and had tasted of the heavenly gift, and were made partakers of [literally, companions with] the Holy Spirit and had tasted the good Word of God [the message of the prophets] and the miracles they had witnessed, if they fell away, to renew them again unto repentance" Hebrews 6:4-6.

If the meaning of the passage is that a person could lose his or her salvation after it was granted, how sad that would be. There is positively no chance of regaining salvation.

Now to the second of the problematic passages mentioned above:

Matthew 10.22-23 states: *"²²All men will hate you because of me, but he who stands firm to the end will be saved. ²³When you are persecuted in one place, flee to another. I tell you the truth, you will not finish going through the cities of Israel before the Son of Man comes."*

Jesus makes this same statement (*he who stands firm to the end will be saved*) in Matthew 24:13 where it is clear that He is referring to a faithful remnant of the Jews during the Tribulation period who refuse to compromise their loyalty to the Lord Jesus Christ. Their endurance shows they are genuine disciples.

Taken by itself, one could interpret the Lord's meaning of that statement in both passages to mean that salvation could be earned or kept by steadfast endurance. It cannot mean this because throughout the Scriptures, salvation is by election, and those elected are kept by the power of God.

Romans 8:28-30 for instance, emphatically states that salvation is by the calling of God, not of one's works.

*"28And we know that in all things God works for the good of those who love him, who have been called according to his purpose. 29For those God foreknew he also predestined to be conformed to the likeness of his Son, that he might be the firstborn among many brothers. 30And those he **predestined**, he also **called;** those he called, he also **justified;** those he justified, he also **glorified."***

Each one of the underlined verbs is in the past tense and denotes a completed action. Those who have been born again have already been glorified in the eyes of God.

In that God cannot fail in the calling (for it is an efficacious call), in that He cannot fail in the predestining, in that He cannot fail in the justifying, in that He cannot fail in the glorifying, we are seen as already with the Lord in heaven. Who is able to prevent it or reverse it? No one, not even one's own self. If it could be done, God is not sovereign. He would be subject to His creation, not His creation to Him.

We have addressed the two passages of Scripture that are most commonly misinterpreted. Now we will consider the eternal security of the believer. 1 Peter 1:1, 2 states:

"¹Peter, an apostle of Jesus Christ, To God's elect, strangers in the world, scattered throughout Pontus, Galatia, Cappadocia, Asia and Bithynia, ²who have been chosen according to the foreknowledge of God the Father, through the sanctifying work of the Spirit, for obedience to Jesus Christ and sprinkling by his blood: Grace and peace be yours in abundance."

By the inspiration of the Holy Spirit, Peter addresses the elect and reminds them that their inheritance is *"incorruptible, undefiled by sin, that fadeth not away, reserved in heaven, kept by the power of God, through faith"* (KJV). Take note of some very interesting words employed by Peter in this passage:

1) Incorruptible, cannot be corrupted by sin.

2) Undefiled, cannot be defiled by sin.

3) Fadeth not away, does not disappear.

4) Kept, held by the power of God.

We are kept by the power of God. This is the divine side. Faith is the human side. Saving faith always has the quality of permanence, as it is God's gift (Ephesians 2:8-9) to those who are His sheep. This faith may be tested, but never lost. It is given from the hand of God.

Much of the confusion about eternal security would be eliminated with a clear understanding of the meaning of grace. Salvation is by grace through faith and not by works. We are not saved because we are good, nor lost because we are bad. A man who is truly born again is safe forever and can be as sure of heaven as if he has already been there ten thousand years. He may fall into sin, and, since the flesh (the fallen nature) of the believer has not been changed and is still corrupt, he may do some evil things. David, for example, was guilty of adultery and murder even though he had been brought into a true relationship with God. He was forgiven for these sins and restored to God's fellowship. However, David suffered greatly as a result of his sins. Every child of God will suffer as a result of the sins he commits.

Though sin must be dealt with, God's grace is not nullified.

If a sinning saint (one who is born again) refuses to confess his sin, God must deal with him. 1 Corinthians 5 demonstrates this principle. Here Paul speaks of a man living in an openly sinful relationship with "his father's wife" (verse 1) – evidently his stepmother. By apostolic judgment, and authority, this man was excluded from the fellowship of the Corinthian church. The church was *"to deliver such an one unto Satan for the destruction of the flesh, that his spirit would be saved in the day of the Lord Jesus"* (verse 5). The apostolic command was: *"Therefore put away from among yourselves that wicked person"* (verse 13). It is evident from 2 Corinthians 2 that by this drastic method, the sinning Christian came back to repentance and confession. We see this in Paul's words in 2 Corinthians 2:5-11:

"⁵If anyone has caused grief, he has not so much grieved me as he has grieved all of you, to some extent—not to put it too severely. ⁶The punishment inflicted on him by the majority is sufficient for him. ⁷Now instead, you ought to forgive and comfort him, so that he will not be over-whelmed by excessive sorrow. ⁸ I urge you, therefore, to reaffirm your love for him. ⁹ The reason I wrote you was to see if you would stand the test and be obedient in everything. ¹⁰ If you forgive anyone, I also forgive him. And what I have forgiven—if there was anything to forgive—I have forgiven in the sight of Christ for your sake, ¹¹ in order that Satan might not

outwit us. For we are not unaware of his schemes."

Paul nowhere implied that the man in His first letter (1 Corinthians 5) or those referred to in his second letter (2 Corinthians 2) lost their salvation. Their sin had to be dealt with, but they themselves remained saved.

Looking at eternal security from another angle:

A long time ago (eternity past) in a far away place (heaven), God the Father and God the Son put into motion those things that would glorify the Godhead. We are given an insight into the heart of God when we hear God the Son pray to the Father: *"You loved me before the foundation of the world"* John 17:24. The three persons of the Godhead (the third being the Holy Spirit) shared a mutual love and fellowship in their eternal counsels.

In these counsels, the Triune God made plans for the universe, including earth and its inhabitants, prior to the creation. *"Known unto God are all His works from the beginning of the world"* Acts 15:18 (KJV). *"Being predestined according to the purpose of Him who works all things after the counsel of His own will."* Ephesians 1:11 (KJV).

In their counsel, they planned for a certain body of people (all persons in every age who would be redeemed) who were *"chosen in Him before the foundation of the world"* Ephesians 1:4. Furthermore, a "book of life" was prepared in which their names were written, although there would be many born "whose names were not written in that book of life" Revelation 17:8.

The Triune God knew that man (His premier creation) would choose to rebel against His will. This resulted in man being cast out of His presence and sentenced to spiritual death, yet He (God), undertook a marvelous plan of redemption for those who would be redeemed. It was agreed that God the Son would become man and endure punishment and separation from God the Father on behalf of man. He was *"foreordained before the foundation of the world"* 1 Peter 1:20 KJV to be *"the Lamb slain from the foundation of the world"* Revelation 13.8 for the payment of man's sin. On the basis of His (the Lamb's) great sacrifice, God could "promise eternal life, before the world began" (Titus 1:2) to all who would come to God the Son as they believed that promise.

It should be stressed, before moving on, that man's salvation and his eternal security is a promise, a pact, between the Godhead. It is an agreement that each would glorify the other as they brought about the salvation of those who were to be redeemed. It should also be stressed that man was not involved in the planning or the carrying out of God's plan.

It must be asked at this point: Could God the Father fail God the Son or the God the Holy Spirit? Could God the Son fail God the Father or God the Holy Spirit? Could God the Holy Spirit fail God the Father or God the Son? The answer, of course, is no. Each one counseled to glorify the other.

John 3:5-8 states that God the Holy Spirit has been and is active among humanity, regenerating many to newness of life for the express purpose of glorifying both the Father and the Son.

"⁵I tell you the truth, no one can enter the kingdom of God unless he is born of water and the Spirit. ⁶Flesh gives birth to flesh, but the Spirit gives birth to spirit. ⁷You should not be surprised at my saying, 'You must be born again.' ⁸The wind blows wherever it pleases. You hear its sound, but you cannot tell where it comes from or where it is going. So it is with everyone born of the Spirit."

We find in this same chapter that God the Father gave God the Son for the salvation of man (John 3:14-17).

"14Just as Moses lifted up the snake in the desert, so the Son of Man must be lifted up, 15that everyone who believes in him may have eternal life. 16"For God so loved the world that he gave his one and only Son, that whoever believes in him shall not perish but have eternal life. 17For God did not send his Son into the world to condemn the world, but to save the world through him."

Also in this same chapter we find that God accepted the sacrifice of God the Son. Consider verses 18-21 and verse 36.

"18Whoever believes in him is not condemned, but whoever does not believe stands condemned already because he has not believed in the name of God's one and only Son. 19This is the verdict: Light has come into the world, but men loved darkness instead of light because their deeds were evil. 20Everyone who does evil hates the light, and will not come into the light for fear that his deeds will be exposed. 21But whoever lives by the truth comes into the light, so that it may be seen plainly that what he has done has been done through God. 36Whoever believes in the Son has eternal life, but whoever rejects the Son will not see life, for God's wrath remains on him."

These verses teach that each member of the Godhead carried out His mission. Each was faithful to the other. This same faithfulness is worked out in the preservation of those who are saved. Consider John 10:25-30:

"25I told you, and ye believed not: the works that I do in my Father's name, they bear witness of me. 26But ye believe not, because ye are not of my sheep, as I said unto you. 27My sheep hear my voice, and I know them, and they follow me: 28And I give unto them eternal life; and they shall never perish, neither shall any man pluck them out of my hand. 29My Father, which gave them me, is greater than all; and no man is able to pluck them out of my Father's hand. 30I and my Father are one."

Eternal life is eternal. Never perish means to <u>never</u> <u>perish</u>. This, according to the passage above, is the emphatic statement of God the Son to the Jews, who were challenging His integrity and claims.

Leaving the Gospel of John we again turn to Romans chapter 8 and reread verses 28-30:

"28And we know that in all things God works for the good of those who love him, who have been called according to his purpose. 29For those God foreknew he also predestined to be

conformed to the likeness of his Son, that he might be the firstborn among many brothers. ³⁰ *And those he predestined, he also called; those he called, he also justified; those he justified, he also glorified."*

God has efficaciously called all those He is conforming to the image of God the Son. Those He called He also justified. Those He justified He also glorified. This calling, justifying, and glorifying are all written in the past tense while said persons are still alive (verse 28). Each one who was predestined, is also called, justified, and glorified in the court of God. None of these are lost.

Returning to the gospel of John, we read: *"*¹¹*I will remain in the world no longer, but they are still in the world, and I am coming to you. Holy Father, protect them by the power of your name—the name you gave me—so that they may be one as we are one.* ¹²*While I was with them, I protected them and kept them safe by that name you gave me. None has been lost except the one doomed to destruction so that Scripture would be fulfilled" John 17:11-12).*

Before His arrest and crucifixion, Jesus thanked the Father for giving His disciples to Him. He states that none were lost except Judas Iscariot (in fulfillment of Scripture). He also asks that these disciples be kept through God the Father's authority (power) and prays for all those who would come to believe in Jesus through the disciple's word. He goes on to pray for all those who would come to believe in Jesus through their (the disciples') word.

17:20-21 *"20 Neither pray I for these alone, but for them also which shall believe on me through their word; 21 That they all may be one; as thou, Father, art in me, and I in thee, that they also may be one in us: that the world may believe that thou hast sent me."*

"Them which shall believe on me" refers also to you and me; we are kept by the same authority that kept the disciples. God cannot fail. He must keep those for whom Jesus died or He would be unfaithful to God the Son and God the Holy Spirit and to their agreement before the creation of the world.

The question is sometimes raised, "What would happen to a sinning Christian if he should die before being brought to repentance and confession? First Corinthians 11:17-34 gives a great answer. Paul wrote: *"17 In the following directives I have no praise for you, for your meetings do more harm than good. 18 In the first place, I hear that when you come* together as a church, there are divisions among you, and to some extent I believe it. ¹⁹No doubt there have to be differences among you to show which of you have God's approval. ²⁰When you come together, it is not the Lord's Supper you eat, ²¹for as you eat, each of you goes ahead without waiting for anybody else. One remains hungry, another gets drunk. ²²Don't you have homes to eat and drink in? Or do you despise the church of God and humiliate those who have nothing? What shall I say to you? Shall I praise you for this? Certainly not! ²³For I received from the Lord what I also passed on to you: The Lord Jesus, on the night he was betrayed, took bread, ²⁴and when he had given thanks, he broke it and said, 'This is my body, which is for you; do this in remembrance of me.' ²⁵In the same way, after supper he took the cup, saying, 'This cup is the new covenant in my blood; do this, whenever you drink it, in remembrance of me.' ²⁶For whenever you eat this bread and drink this cup, you proclaim the Lord's death until he comes. ²⁷Therefore, whoever eats the bread or drinks the cup of the Lord in an unworthy manner will be guilty of sinning against the body and blood of the Lord. ²⁸A man ought to examine himself before he eats of the bread and drinks of the cup. ²⁹For anyone who eats and drinks without recognizing the body of the Lord eats and drinks judgment on himself. ³⁰That is why many among you are weak and sick, and a number of you have fallen asleep. ³¹But if we judged ourselves, we would *not come under judgment. [32]When we are judged by the Lord, we are being disciplined so that we will not be condemned with the world. [33]So then, my brothers, when you come together to eat, wait for each other. [34]If anyone is hungry, he should eat at home, so that when you meet together it may not result in judgment. And when I come I will give further directions."*

In the Corinthian church, many were sick, and some had even died because they did not rightly judge and conduct themselves respectfully toward their Christian brothers or the Lord. Because they did not judge themselves, the Lord brought chastisement and even death in order that they "be not condemned with the world" (verse 32).

In closing, perhaps there are some who lack an assurance of their eternal security. It may be that their doubt is not in God's ability to sustain them, but in the assurance that they were once truly saved. It is very probable that they question whether they truly repented of their sins, took up their cross, and followed Jesus because they fell back into sin. Second Peter 2:10 warns us to *"give diligence to make your calling and election sure: for if ye do these things, ye shall never fall."* Each of us should confirm our call and election, as Peter exhorts his readers.

There are two facets of God's plan of salvation. **Election** refers to His sovereign pre-creation choice of individuals. **Call** refers to His action in time by which the choice is made evident. One's election took place before the world was made; His or her call takes place when he or she is converted. Chronologically, election comes first, then call. In human experience; however, one first becomes aware of his call, then realizes he was chosen in Christ in eternity past. One cannot make his call and election surer than God's grace; God's eternal purpose can never be thwarted.

Doubt of salvation sometimes comes when one falls back into sin. One can avoid such consternation by growing in the likeness of Christ, which is a confirmation of salvation. Manifesting the fruit of the Spirit is unmistakable evidence that he or she truly belongs to Him. A holy life proves the reality of one's salvation.

However, even as God's children we all sin. First John 1:8-9 states emphatically: *"[8]If we say that we have no sin, we deceive ourselves, and the truth is not in us. [9]If we confess our sins, he is faithful and just to forgive us our sins, and to cleanse us from all unrighteousness."*

When one commits sin, (which one will, regretfully), he or she need not fear the loss of salvation. On the contrary, evidence of the surety of salvation is in the truth of the recognition of said sin and a desire of its confession and cleansing.

Peter refers to those scattered throughout Pontus, Galatia, Cappadocia, Asia, and Bithynia as the elect. *"¹Peter, an apostle of Jesus Christ, To God's elect, strangers in the world, scattered throughout Pontus, Galatia, Cappadocia, Asia and Bithynia, ²who have been chosen according to the foreknowledge of God the Father, through the sanctifying work of the Spirit, for obedience to Jesus Christ and sprinkling by his blood: Grace and peace be yours in abundance"* 1 Peter 1:1-2.

Then he adds in verses 3-5:

"³Praise be to the God and Father of our Lord Jesus Christ! In his great mercy he has given us new birth into a living hope through the resurrection of Jesus Christ from the dead, ⁴and into an inheritance that can never perish, spoil or fade—kept in heaven for you, ⁵who through faith are shielded by God's power until the coming of the salvation that is ready to be revealed in the last time."

We are kept by the power of God; that is the divine side. Faith is the human side. Saving faith always has the quality of permanence because it is God's gift to those who are His sheep. Because faith is from the hand of God, it may be tested but never lost. Praise God, we are secure. We have this promise because God keeps us secure and because God the Father, God the Son, and God the Holy Spirit are faithful to one another.

Have you, dear reader, trusted in Jesus for your right standing before God? He said: *"I am the way, the truth and the life, no one comes to the Father but by me" John 14:6.* Each of us should pause and ask ourselves: Is there evidence (see pages 112-115) in my life that I am truly a child of God? Am I truly spiritually born again? It is imperative that one is a child of God, for if one is not, at death, he or she will be eternally separated from Him. Jesus warned in Matthew 25:41:

"Then he will say to those on his left, 'Depart from me, you who are cursed, into the eternal fire prepared for the devil and his angels.'"

May God richly bless you! Hope to see you in heaven.

About the Book

Many people today would list many different things as being man's dilemma; such things as: health problems, unemployment, poverty, crime, war, and so on. Each, of course, are problems found in every society, excluding none. One could say man's dilemma is universal and they would be correct. However, each of the things listed above are actually the result of man's dilemma, not the cause. The cause is found in man's depravity. In that depravity, every un-regenerated human being sets his own standard as to his or her conduct of life. Man has rejected the absolute standard of his creator and as a result is alienated toward not only God, but from one another. Man has no solution for this and therein lies the dilemma. God on the other hand, has the solution, it is found in His provision, the Lord Jesus Christ. In the pages of this work the author considers man's dilemma God's solution from eleven different perspectives. Each chapter is a study in itself but fits nicely as one completed work.

May God bless His Word to the reader's understanding as he or she meditates on it.

Note: The reader will notice that many Bible passages have been repeated in several chapters. The writer found this necessary to bring out the complete message of each chapter.